Are Not My People Worthy?

Are Not My People Worthy?

THE STORY OF

Matthew 25: Ministries

Wendell E. Mettey

Providence House Publishers

PROVIDENCE PUBLISHING CORPORATION

FRANKLIN, TENNESSEE

Scripture quotations marked "NIV" are taken from HOLY BIBLE, NEW INTERNATIONAL VERSION®. Copyright © 1973, 1978, 1984 by International Bible Society. Used by permission of Zondervan Publishing House.

Scripture quotations marked "RSV" are taken from Revised Standard Version of the Bible, copyright 1952 [2nd edition, 1971] by the Division of Christian Education of the National Council of the Churches of Christ in the United States of America. Used by permission. All rights reserved.

Printed in the United States of America

08   07   06   05   04   1   2   3   4   5

Library of Congress Control Number: 2004106324

ISBN: 1-57736-321-3

Cover design and illustration by Hope Seth

PROVIDENCE HOUSE PUBLISHERS
an imprint of
Providence Publishing Corporation
238 Seaboard Lane • Franklin, Tennessee 37067
www.providence-publishing.com
800-321-5692

This book is written to the glory of God and dedicated to the One who touched me that night in my apartment, calling me to fulfill Matthew 25:34–40.

Contents

Acknowledgments

The song by Rodgers and Hammerstein, "You'll Never Walk Alone," has certainly been true for my life. While my walk has often been difficult and sometimes lonely, I can honestly say I have never walked alone. God has always walked with me. I have also had the company of many wonderful people. In this limited space, I wish to acknowledge and thank those who have walked with me and contributed greatly to the writing of this book.

Thank you Mickey, you are the love of my life and my best friend; Mom and Dad, for your example of love and caring for those in need; my three wonderful children and their spouses: Tim and Chanin Mettey, Clare and Michael Iery, and Aaron Mettey. My grandchildren, who have me completely under their control: Olivia, Ethan, and Cora. My brothers and sister: Joe, who showed me strength; Tom (and wife, Vonnie), who showed me compassion; Anita, who showed me friendship; and my late sister-in-law,

Joan Mettey, who showed me kindness; and "Granny," whose home was a refuge from the storms of life. Mickey's parents, Harry and Kate Keller, for loving me like a son; and Paul and Sheila Keller and Larry and Marilyn Keller for loving me like a brother.

Thank you: Dr. Cowley, for being my pastor for twenty-seven years and greatly influencing my life; the loving people of the churches I served: the Walnut Hills Baptist Church, Montgomery Community Baptist Church, and truly a servant congregation—the Church of Matthew 25 and its elders (not including those mentioned later): Mike Elam, Bob Harrison, Stacy Creamer, Jane Burke, and Lisa Elfers; "Living Epistles," who are now with the Lord: Bert Stringer, Jean Hoskins, Thelma Jarvis, Walter Johnson, and the Reverend Dr. Charles Stewart; and my best friend and colleague, the late Rev. Dr. Michael Brandy, who was Matthew 25: Ministries' most enthusiastic cheerleader and someone who taught us so much about living by the way he faced dying.

Thank you, Michael Brandy Jr. and David Knust—your passion and commitment have played a significant role in the success of Matthew 25: Ministries; Shannon Carter and Dick Bere, dear friends and partners in helping needy school children. Bill and Esaf Meyer, my brother and sister in the Lord. My longtime secretary and best "buddy," Mary Martin. Harry Yeaggy, whose friendship I cherish. The Reverend Larry Sprinkle, my mentor and friend.

Special thanks to the U.S. Air Force Reserve units scattered throughout the United States: the 445th Air Wing and the 88th Transportation Squadron at Wright Patterson Air Force Base in Dayton, Ohio; the 433rd Air Wing at

Kelley Air Force Base in San Antonio, Texas; and the 756th Airlift Squadron at Andrews Air Force Base in Maryland. Special thanks to my good friend, Lt. Col. Karl McGregor, who kept the Matthew 25: Ministries' dream alive. Geoff Slagle for assistance with early airlifts, Jana Widmeyer and U.S. Senator Mike DeWine for their support and concern for the poor, and Adm. Jeremiah Denton for his service to our country and his legislative initiative, which created the Denton Program.

Thank you, Axel and Sherly Sobalvarro, whose 1989 visit to our home actually began Matthew 25: Ministries, and for all of your faithful work in receiving and distributing supplies in Nicaragua. Alvaro Pereida, executive director of the American Nicaraguan Foundation (ANF), my brother in the Lord, friend and co-laborer in reaching the poor. Lilliam Aguilla and staff at the ANF warehouse in Nicaragua. Norma Hanna, who gave up her comfortable life in the United States and returned to Nicaragua to work and live among the poor. William Abdalah, M.D., and his family who gave early support to our work. Margarita Caldera, secretary general of education, and Dr. Jose Antonio Alvarado, minister of education for the Nicaraguan government, both greatly assisted Matthew 25: Ministries in reaching thousands of needy school children. Tony Barbeiri of Food For The Poor, and Brian Brown of NRC for their crucial partnership. Rodger and Beverly Stanfield, Scott and Rhonda Miller, Rich and Jennifer Housh, for their continuous support from the beginning.

Thank you to our many volunteers who come faithfully to the warehouse and sort, box, and palletize supplies. Those who have been with me from the beginning: Lee and

June Keeling; Lillian Smith; Jim Baldus; Lucille and Bob Marcello; and Lillian and Ray Black. Two of our most faithful volunteers, Karl and Trish Hauck. The many churches, clubs, companies, families, scout troops, civic groups and schools who volunteer, especially the Hamilton First Baptist Church in Ohio, led by the Reverend Bill and Bert Brandingham and the First Presbyterian Church of Harrison, Ohio, led by Dr. Richard and Carol Morris. Others whose support has been significant: Mary and T. J. Estell; Jim and Francie Russell; Nancy and Vic Buzachero; and Ed and Jeanette Crain, friends and encouragers. Our many churches, individuals, and groups who support our work with the poor through their financial giving.

Thanks to the many who have traveled with me to Nicaragua. Particularly, Mike Staudinger, M.D., who, when most are thinking about retiring, gave up a successful veterinarian practice to become a medical doctor. Mike, your passion to heal the sick has been truly an inspiration. Glenn Grismere, good friend and supporter of Matthew 25: Ministries. Jim Fidler, M.D., who is indeed the "good physician." Fred Pottschmidt, my faithful friend, and favorite student; Doug Thomson, who provided our first office and located our first real warehouse; the Reverend Vernon "Pete" Hood, my lifelong friend and co-laborer in the Kingdom. My wonderful staff: Patty Dilg, who has been with me since I taught her in Sunday school; Anita Bowman, the best thing to happen to our volunteers; Brian Bertke, Don Marcello, John Canfield, Tim Mettey, Tina Schrenker, Don Olson, Paula Marcello, John Marker, Dick Dostal, Fred Hansberger, Joodi Archer, the late Paul Francis (called by the American Indians of North Dakota, "the man who loved Indians"); and Jayne Wessel who read my scribble and typed the final manuscript.

My supportive Board of Directors: Sandie and Dan Bloomfield, Jerry Francis, Michael Brandy Jr., Chuck Burke, Esly Caldwell, M.D., Judy Caldwell, Glenn Grismere, Rich Housh, David Knust, Rhonda Miller, Sally Phelps, Michael Staudinger, M.D., Douglas Thomson, Esq., Harry Yeaggy, and Joe Wambach (Emeritus). Past directors: Rick Dostal whose "can do" spirit was contagious and Al Meyer, friend and fellow sojourner to Nicaragua. Those who have given valuable professional service: Justice and Young Advertising; Linda Gill, C.P.A.; and Eugene J. Martin, appraisal assistance. The Blue Ash/Montgomery and the Mason Deerfield Rotary Clubs for their financial assistance and support in building in Nicaragua a vocational school and a regional feeding center.

To over eighty corporations and hospitals who donate products to Matthew 25: Ministries and the wonderful people who make these companies great. To mention only a few: Eric Boeckley, who gave us our first truckload of hospital linens; Carl DeBlasio, who provided our first moving van; Nick Kaluger, our first five semi-loads of school supplies; and Greg Burchett, who has kept the trucks coming; Tami and Rachael Longaberger, whose first fifteen truckloads of fabric helped us supply thousands of sewing centers; Cindy Wingert, who helped us establish a system for handling corporate product returns; Paul Heiman, whose life and story of narrowly escaping the Nazi concentration camps greatly inspires; the Sanford Corporation for our first shipment of pencils and Will Wilson for keeping the pencils coming; and a special friend of Matthew 25:

Ministries and the poor, Scott Farmer. Thank you Scott and the Cintas Corporation, for your support and partnership in reaching the needy.

I would also like to thank John Donohoo, Audrey Ayers, Kevin Marinacci, Tom Faig, Carl Marquette Jr., Lee Arrasmith, Herb and Joy Nichols, Karen Schwarz, Jeff Rower, Cindy and Mark Hallen, Lisa and Joe Elfers, Mark Creamer, Jean Brandy, Cousin Joan Mettey, Jim and Robin Hobold, Jenny Harrison, Paul Smith, Don Heithaus, Ann Barfels, and Richard Filisky, my dear brother in the Lord.

I wish to thank those who are not mentioned due to space constraints and memory fatigue. God knows your names and the poor of the world know of your good deeds. There have been so many of you. Forgive me if your name doesn't appear.

And lastly, those whom this book is all about, the "least of these." I have had the privilege of knowing and serving you. You have given me more than I could ever give you. The courageous way you face the enormous challenges of daily living strengthens my resolve to do all I can so that "you'll never walk alone."

Introduction: Aiming for the Heart

No sooner had Anne concluded her remarks than her movie-star husband, Kirk Douglas, sprang to his feet and rushed across the stage. At eighty-seven, he still had a commanding stage presence and, apparently, had not lost his fondness for being in front of an audience. Wrapping her up in his arms, he leaned into the microphone and said, "Isn't she wonderful!" He then proceeded to give his leading lady of forty-nine years a big kiss. The audience responded with thunderous applause.

As the Douglases were returning to their seats, Corbin Bernsen, television actor and producer, stepped to the podium to introduce the next recipient. I took a deep breath and glanced at the program. *One, two, three recipients ahead of me. Good*, I thought. *The Douglases would be a hard act to follow!* Besides, I was still pinching myself to see if I was dreaming. There I was, on stage at the Kennedy Center, sitting next to "Spartacus" and surrounded by

nationally known people who had distinguished themselves in the entertainment industry, the political arena,
and corporate America—the *Who's Who* in America. I was
not only sitting among them, but in a few minutes I would
be called to speak to them and to a theater full of the
unsung heroes, all those who had been invited to
Washington to receive the Jefferson Award for Public
Service. When my turn came, what was I going to say and
how would I say it in the three minutes given to each of
the recipients?

On the way to the Kennedy Center that morning, my
wife, Mickey, and I shared an elevator with Sam Beard, the
president and cofounder of the American Institute of
Public Service, the organization sponsoring the ceremonies. Sipping hot coffee and eating a napkin-wrapped
danish, he looked at me and said, "Reverend Mettey, keep
it short and aim for the heart!" I kept repeating his advice
over and over, especially the part about aiming for the
heart. No one was adhering to the three minute rule. One
of the recipients went on for over twenty minutes. Almost
last in the program, I knew I had to keep it short—no
problem—but aim for the heart?

I closed my eyes and prayed, *Lord, help me aim for the
heart!* With that prayer the entire Matthew 25: Ministries
experience flashed before my eyes.

Chapter One

In the Trenches

In the summer of 1980, I was the pastor of a vibrant, diverse inner-city congregation, the Walnut Hills Baptist Church. Mickey and I had three children: Tim, six; Clare, five; and our youngest, Aaron, was almost two. While attending the University of Cincinnati thirteen years before, I served the church as the youth director. It was also the church in which I grew up. After graduation in 1968, I continued as the youth director while taking a job with the Hamilton County Welfare Department as a caseworker. The district assigned to me was "ground zero" of the race riots which had ended the previous year. Caseworker safety was a major concern of the Department. During orientation, we were given our orders on how and when we could enter our districts. When I started in 1968, things had quieted down but the tension and scars still remained. Burned-out buildings and abandoned storefronts lined the streets. I never felt threatened, however, because I had grown up a neighborhood away.

My caseload consisted of about a hundred households. A majority of my households were single mothers with children. They were referred to as Aid to Dependent Children (ADC) households. I also had clients, as the Welfare Department called them, who were classified as Aid to the Blind (AB), Aid to the Aged (AA), and clients who received short-term assistance, classified as General Relief (GR). The primary job of caseworkers was to visit their clients in their homes and determine if they were still eligible for public assistance. Eligibility Determinations, as they were called, were done once a year for AB and AA, twice a year for ADC, and every three months for GR clients. Every household had a large file of these eligibility reports and other pertinent information. Caseworkers spent most of their time making these files larger. Unfortunately, caseworkers did very little social work.

The average stay for a caseworker at the Welfare Department was three to six months! Idealistic and fresh from college, they thought they were going to make a huge difference in the lives of their clients and do it in a short period of time. They left as quickly as they came, disillusioned and blaming the system for their failure. What else, it was the '60s. The caseworkers who grew up in the inner city, as I did, had an advantage over those who were raised in the suburbs. We knew the realities of inner-city life because we lived them every day growing up. We were more realistic and streetwise.

My clients were primarily African-American. This was my first real exposure to the black community; until this time, I had never been in a black person's home. During my brief but intense fifteen months at the Welfare Department, I was able to confront personal prejudices and dispel stereotypes and came away with a greater appreciation for most I met.

During my time at the Department, I saw clients face enormous obstacles yet hold on tenaciously to the goodness of God. They knew how to laugh and enjoy life, especially when life was hurting the most and when it was anything but enjoyable. I encountered a wisdom among my clients which one could not get from a book or some ivy-covered school; a wisdom which grew out of their life struggles. I'm not sure who said it first, but if the difference between success and failure is simply getting up one more time than we are knocked down, then I met a lot of successful people. I took away from my days as a caseworker many valuable lessons which would personally help me later in life.

Chapter Two

A Good Idea Gone Bad

During my Welfare Department days I began to see major flaws in the way we were seeking to help the poor. I was front-row-center and cheering the loudest when President Lyndon B. Johnson presented his famous March 16, 1964, message to Congress. He opened the speech with, "Because it is right, because it is wise, and because for the first time in our history it is possible to conquer poverty." With that he declared the unconditional "War on Poverty." I was one of the first to enlist and become one of its most loyal soldiers.

The objective of the war was well defined—eliminate poverty that was affecting thirty-five million Americans. The plan was simple—give the poor money, free medical care, and housing. Along with the money and services came programs such as VISTA, Neighborhood Youth Corps, Job Corps, and Head Start. The bureaucracy that administered all of this grew enormously. Serving on the front lines each day, I began to see people become dependent on the Department and, again, upon the very system seeking to make them independent. Case file after case file revealed a cyclical pattern of generational dependence on Welfare. It was seen as a right of passage for a teen to have a child out of wedlock, get assigned her own caseworker, and receive her own Welfare check.

The system was also destroying the traditional family consisting of a mother and father with children. A single woman with a child or children received immediate Welfare assistance; but a couple with children could only qualify for temporary, minimal assistance. There was even a name for this—MIC, "Man in the Case." This meant there was an unclaimed father/husband/man living with the ADC family. We had caseworkers make unannounced visits to the home hoping to catch a MIC. (Caseworkers would even look under beds and in closets.) If a MIC was found, the family could lose their welfare. We were not only creating dependency on the system and trashing the family, we were taking away incentives. The Welfare Department became the company store; our clients became so dependent on it, financially, psychologically, and culturally, they would never be able to break free.

I also saw a growing resentment among the poor. The "War on Poverty" promised more than it could deliver and raised unrealistic expectations. It made getting out of poverty sound so easy. Well, it was anything but easy. Failed attempts caused people to turn on the system. There were many who abused or took advantage of every attempt to help them. In the fifteen months I was there, I was only able to help one courageous mother of five receive her nursing degree and get off of Welfare.

One afternoon on my way back to the Welfare Department, I stopped by the church building. My pastor was there and we had an impromptu meeting in the hallway. He raised the possibility of me going to seminary. A few months later, he accompanied Mickey and me to the seminary which he had graduated from in 1927. That August, Mickey and I moved into seminary housing and I began a three-year Master of Divinity program.

My intention was to receive a dual masters degree in social work and divinity that was offered jointly with the nearby university. I found myself, however, moving away from social work and concentrating more on my divinity studies. This was due primarily to the influence of my professors. For three years I felt as if I were sitting at the feet of the apostles. They opened up the Bible to me in many applicable and relevant ways.

It was three memorable years for both of us. After graduation we came back to the Walnut Hills Baptist Church in Cincinnati, and I became the associate pastor with an emphasis on community work. Dr. Arthur Cowley, who had been at the church for thirty-five years, was my mentor.

Dr. Cowley was certainly colorful. He came alone to the United States from England when he was fifteen years old, carrying the reputation of being the "boy preacher." Handbills carrying his likeness and the time and place of when "little Arthur" would preach were posted throughout London, England. People flocked to these tent revival services to hear him. They were amazed at his maturity, delivery, and understanding of the Bible. Many responded to the call to give their lives to Christ and few went away disappointed. Overcoming many obstacles, Dr. Cowley's purpose in coming to the United States was realized in 1927, when his seminary awarded him a Ph.D. In 1937, he came to the church where he would serve as pastor until his passing. He was a remarkable human being who became an institution in the community during his lifetime. He was the only pastor I had ever known, and he significantly influenced my life.

Chapter Three

"Splanchnizomai"

I never thought that what I was doing was social work, nor did I ever think of myself as a social worker. My undergraduate degree was in economics. I had not even taken a social work course while in college. To me, what I was doing was merely an expression of my Christianity or perhaps the evidence of it. I was drawn to such New Testament passages as 1 John 3:17 (NIV): "If anyone has material possessions and sees his brother in need but has no pity on him, how can the love of God be in him?" And James 2:14 (NIV): "What good is it, my brothers, if a man claims to have faith but has no deeds? Can such faith save him? Suppose a brother or sister is without clothes or daily food. If you say to him 'Go, I wish you well, keep warm and well fed,' but does nothing about his physical needs what good is it (faith). In the same way faith by itself, if it is not accompanied by action is dead."

As a child I was taught by my parents in both word and deed that God was concerned about the whole person. The idea that there existed a dichotomy between the body and soul was completely foreign to me. While I was taught that Jesus came to redeem a lost world, it was also pointed out that he stopped repeatedly on his way to Calvary to help people spiritually, yes, but also physically and emotionally.

We are told that Jesus healed large gatherings of people (Matt. 4:23; Mark 1:34; and Luke 4:40). There were also twenty-three occasions in which Jesus healed thirty-five individuals. It is interesting to note that while some of these people had serious illnesses such as leprosy and mental illness, most did not. For instance, He healed a man with a shriveled hand. One healing could possibly be classified as cosmetic. This healing occurred when He healed Malchus, the servant of the high priest, after the apostle Peter severed his ear.

Why would Jesus heal a person with leprosy one day when the next the person could die of heart failure or contract a deadly disease? Why did Jesus constantly interrupt His eternal mission with these temporal acts of healing? Why did He not say to the possessed and the dispossessed, the poor and hungry, the blind and the lame, "You gotta learn to 'tough it out.' Your pain and misery, like life, are only temporary. Remember God loves you," pat the person on the head, then walk on? Why did Jesus stop to help so many people?

To answer these questions we need to look to the word "compassion". To understand compassion we need to look to the Greek language, the original language of the New Testament.

The Greek word for compassion is *"splanchnizomai"*. It is the strongest Greek word for pity. Its root meaning comes from the word *"splanchna"* which means "the bowels." To the ancient Greeks the seat of emotion was not in the heart but in the bowels. When we look closely at where and in what context this word is used in the New Testament, we arrive at the following definition: "Compassion is that 'gut wrenching' feeling we experience when we see another human being suffering, which then motivates us to take action to end or alleviate the suffering."

The gospel writers tell of five specific occasions when this word is used—all describe Jesus. Why only five? There certainly were more than five occasions when Jesus was moved with compassion. I believe the writers of the Gospels selected these occasions from the many to show the areas of human suffering which are of greatest concern to God and, therefore, should be for us.

On the first occasion the large crowd of people who gathered around Jesus moved Him deeply. Jesus had stood before many crowds and was not so moved. There was something different about this one. Being physically exhausted from a very demanding travel schedule and emotionally drained by the masses that descended upon Him daily, pleading with Him to fix what was broken in their lives could have added to it. Whatever it was, we are told that when He looked upon this particular crowd, "He had compassion on them because they were harassed or *troubled* and helpless or *scattered* like sheep without a shepherd" (Matt. 9:36).

The Greeks had thirteen words for the verb "to trouble". The word used here is *"skullo"* which means "to flay." To Jesus their pain and suffering could be compared to being skinned alive! The word "scattered" comes from the Greek "*rhipto*" which means to be "thrown or cast down." They were wondering about aimlessly, "like sheep without a shepherd," troubled, cast down, and lost!

Second, there was the leper who fell at Jesus' feet, pleading for mercy. Lepers were the walking dead in Jesus' day. They were sentenced to a lifetime of isolation and loneliness, abandoned by society, never again to be touched or embraced. People were so afraid of catching the disease, lepers were forbidden to come within a certain distance of people. They were banished from any form of human interaction, except with other lepers. They were totally at the mercy of the community for the basic necessities of their pitiful existence. Seeing this man and hearing his plea to be cleansed so that he could return to his loved ones and the life he once knew, Jesus was "filled with compassion" (Mark 1:41 NIV). Jesus then did the unthinkable, He touched him before He healed him. In doing so, I believe Jesus was making a statement.

When someone was healed the Greek word "*iaomai*" would be used. But when the leper was healed the word "*katharizo*" was used which meant "to be made clean." Jesus was saying in His touch that no one is unclean before God. No one is untouchable!

On the third occasion, another crowd had gathered around Jesus. Many had traveled for miles and followed Jesus for three days. Their numbers exceeded ten thousand men, women, and children. Their time with Jesus left them refreshed spiritually, but physically hungry. Thinking that the crowd might turn on them when it was discovered that no provisions were made to feed them, the disciples tried to send them home and make a quick exit. Jesus did not care for this game plan at all. He did not see the crowd as a potential threat or danger. It was an opportunity to show how God was concerned for the whole person. He said, "I have compassion on the crowd" (Matt. 15:32 NIV), and performed the only miracle recorded in all four Gospels, the feeding of the multitude with a few fish and loaves of bread.

The fourth occasion happened on that ancient Jericho road. Two blind beggars could not believe their good fortune when they heard Jesus walking by. They called out, but those around Jesus pushed them away and told them to be quiet. But they shouted even louder. They would not be denied this opportunity. What a pathetic sight—arms flailing, heads shaking, matted hair, dirty faces, pushed and shoved—a few in the crowd no doubt found it humorous, most found them disgraceful. Jesus saw it as neither. He pushed the crowd aside and "(having) compassion on them touched their eyes" (Matt. 20:34 NIV). Before Jesus healed them, He asked them a question: "What do you want me to do for you?" They did not say, "give us our sight" or "help us see again." They said in unison, "Lord, let our eyes be opened!" Their great pain did not come from being blind, but from what being blind took from them. It closed off the world to them.

The fifth and last recorded time Jesus was moved with compassion was perhaps the saddest occasion of all. Jesus and the disciples came upon a funeral procession. Someone had died, a resident of the little town of Nain. Walking alone behind the casket was a widow who was burying her only son. Without a husband or son she now had absolutely no standing in the community. She was totally disenfranchised and at the mercy of the townspeople. Mercy didn't seem too promising coming from such a small town. She was better off than the leper and the blind, but not by much. On the occasion of her son's death, society would dispose of her because of something which she could not control. She became the dispossessed. We are told that "His (Jesus') heart went out to her." He was moved by compassion and raised her son to life (Luke 7:13).

On these five occasions we see how Jesus was filled with compassion for the crowds who were troubled and physically hungry, those shunned by society, the untouchables, those closed off from the world, and, finally, the dispossessed.

There is no question that Jesus pointed people towards the eternal, the "here after," but He lived and reached out to people in the "here and now." We see in these acts of compassion that it does matter to Jesus how we treat one another and it especially matters how we treat the disadvantaged. We not only see this arising out of these acts of healing and compassion, but we see it throughout His life.

He confronted those in authority who mistreated people, "Woe to you teachers of the law and Pharisees, you hypocrites" (Matt. 22:13). He also attacked the corrupt system which was taking advantage of the people when He overturned the money changers in the temple, saying they were a "den of robbers" (Matt. 21:12–13). He constantly went after a religious system which was big on show but neglected the more important matters of, ". . . justice, mercy, and faithfulness" (Matt. 23:23).

Jesus broke down racial barriers (John 4). He was an advocate for children (Mark 9:36; 10:13–16); for the oppressed, "(You) teachers tie up heavy loads and put them on men's shoulders, but then you are unwilling to lift a finger to move them" (Matt. 23:4); and for the victimized (John 8:1–11).

Jesus condemned a society that honored the rich man who lived in the proverbial lap of luxury while ignoring poor Lazarus who, covered with sores, begged at the rich man's gate everyday (Luke 16:19). What kind of society would be so "uncompassionate" that neither the rich man nor any other passersby would help such a poor soul?

Jesus did not see souls walking around, he saw people. The same people we see, complete with skin and bones, emotions, daily trouble, worries, illnesses, and, yes, of course, an eternal soul. With Jesus it was never either/or, it was always both/and. I was not a caseworker because of some theological statement I wished to make. It was simply that my "guts" ached when I saw someone suffering and all I could think of was finding a way to end or, at least, relieve the suffering.

Chapter Four

Discovering What it Means to Be a Servant Church

Mickey and I came to Walnut Hills Baptist Church fresh from seminary in June of 1972. That August, Dr. Cowley developed heart problems and died some weeks later. Needless to say, we were all shocked. An era had come to an end; a man many relied upon was gone. Before he died, he called a church trustee to his bedside. Dr. Cowley dictated his last message to the church he loved. In those deathbed dictations, he expressed the wish that the church call me to succeed him as pastor. The church, nor I, could do otherwise. A week after his funeral the church extended to me an invitation to be the pastor. I accepted. How quickly things in life can change. The words of the psalmist were certainly true, "As for man, his days are like grass, he flourishes like a flower of the field; the wind blows over it and it is gone, and its place remembers it no more" (Ps. 103:15–16 NIV).

What in the world am I doing here? I asked myself countless times during that first year. The weekly preaching

(*How did I manage to graduate from seminary without a single preaching course?*), the lack of experience in dealing with the inner dynamics of church life and personalities, facing the daily realities of an aging and declining inner-city church, grieving over the loss of a dearly loved pastor, and trying to fill his shoes; all of the above raised serious questions as to my sanity of accepting this position. If Mickey and I did not believe that God, not only the church, had called us, I would have resigned.

In God's good time the church began to travel a different path. The comparisons between Dr. Cowley and me became fewer. Those who were waiting for him to retire so they could leave, did. Gradually, we gained our equilibrium and changes began to occur. We began to cast off the last vestiges of those glorious days of the 1950s when it was standing-room-only at the morning service. We took a hard look at who we were and the ministry to which God had called us. We stopped raiding our small-and-shrinking endowment fund and began "paying as we go." We focused on the community immediately around us—identifying it as our ministry area—and explored the meaning of being the Servant Church. The church was becoming the new wineskin Jesus talked about, and our renewed enthusiasm, new ideas, and members were the new wine.

The church was a fascinating collection of people. Sitting in the congregation on Sunday mornings were those with graduate degrees, others employed as professionals, and some with sixth-grade educations who did mostly domestic work. Looking to Jesus, I discovered that the best way of communicating the gospel to such a diverse Sunday-morning congregation was putting the message in stories. Everyone can relate to a story and find meaning in it for their lives. The worship on Sundays was powerful. We had one of the finest choirs anywhere. Seldom did we leave the Sunday-morning service without feeling the presence of God.

One brief episode gives the flavor of the neighborhood people who attended on Sunday morning and thought of Walnut Hills as their church home. The congregation was loving and accepting of all who came. As a result, God began sending us the "street people," as they were called, many of whom were mentally ill. A man named Ray believed that God had called him to preach the Word. He could often be seen on street corners preaching away and handing out pamphlets which made sense only to Ray and perhaps the good Lord. Our ushers stood in the back of the sanctuary during the entire Sunday service looking for any unusual behavior. They kept one eye closed and one eye opened during the morning prayer because we had so many people who could be unpredictable. On this particular day, however, both eyes must have been shut.

During the morning prayer I felt the presence of something, and I didn't think it was angelic in nature. I opened one eye and there was Ray quietly standing in front of the pulpit, staring up at me. I came to a fast, "amen." I went down the chancel steps and asked him what he wanted. By this time, two ushers were halfway down the side aisle. I waved them off. Ray told me that God had instructed him to preach at the service that day. I said without thinking, "Well, Ray, He told me the same thing and I was here first." That made perfect sense to Ray, thank God. He voluntarily went back to his seat and never asked to preach again.

Chapter Five

When the Solution Becomes the Problem

Growing up in the inner city and being a pastor of an inner-city church in the 1970s did much to shape my philosophy and attitude regarding the poor. First, let me say, being poor is not just the lack of money. Poverty is multifaceted. It is a mindset and can become a way of life. It is about how a person defines himself and perceives the world around him. It is a matter of being exposed to the bigger world and the level at which one sets his sights. Breaking the chains of poverty can be done—many have done so—but it demands sacrifice, determination, hard work, and, I believe, a little help! That's where I felt called—to help people lift themselves out of poverty.

My goal was to help people better their lives and discover the full potential given them by a great and loving God. There were many programs available to accomplish this. To me they were all measured by a very pragmatic question—"Did they work?" At the end of the day, has one poor person become "unpoor"?

With the exception of a few programs, the answer was a resounding, "No!" Sadly, instead of liberating people from poverty, we were making matters worse. There were two main reasons.

The first was doing for people, instead of helping them to do for themselves. I was constantly contacted by people who wanted to help the poor. Most were sincere; many, however, felt guilty that they had so much and the poor had so little. I suppose they wanted absolution and a quick "feel-good" fix. They weren't in it for the right reasons or for the long haul. They wanted to create some Norman Rockwell situation—with some loose change and spare time, change a life. They would often decide what the person or family needed, and then proceeded to do it for them. One person complained to me once, "There we were painting their kitchen and they were in the other room watching television!" Inevitably, these situations would always end in disappointment and further the stereotypes of the poor.

The second reason was feeling sorry for people. This is the worst thing anyone can do. Feeling sorry for someone diminishes expectations, removes all accountability, justifies any situation or behavior, and eliminates any objective measurement for determining if you are helping the person. We are not to feel sorry for the poor, we are to help the poor!

There is a huge difference between compassion and feeling sorry for someone. We saw earlier how, when Jesus was moved by compassion, He reached out to help people by removing the predicament in which they found themselves. Jesus never said when moved by compassion, say to a man with a crippled leg, "Come and I'll carry you around for the rest of your life." He healed the man so he could walk around by himself. We can't heal as Jesus did, but we can help the man get physical therapy or a leg brace if needed, help him find a job, and the bus route to the job.

Chapter Six

The Golden Rule of Compassion

The passage of Scripture called the "Golden Rule" is perhaps the most quoted and best known of the entire Bible. A version of it appears in Judaism, Hinduism, Buddhism, and even Confucianism. We do not know who gave it the name "Golden Rule", but we can trace its origins to the mid-eighteenth century.

Jesus gave us the Golden Rule during His famous "Sermon on the Mount" when he said, ". . . do unto others as you would have them do unto you" (Matt. 7:12 NIV). Some have said this was the climax of His sermon because, after giving us this principle to live by, He said it is "the sum of all the prophets and the Law." In other words, when it is all said and done, this is how we are to treat others.

There is no other person in all of literature who lived the Golden Rule better than the man called the "Good Samaritan". The Gospel writers recorded forty parables or stories told by Jesus. One of the most familiar and popular is the story of "The Good Samaritan." As with all of Jesus' stories, the Good Samaritan comes right out of the morning news. "Man beaten and robbed—left for dead on dangerous JJ highway. Pictures at eleven." Also Jesus' stories are not lofty theological discourses, seeking to convey an esoteric concept. They are simple stories containing profound truths for everyday living. Such is the story of the Good Samaritan.

Now let us see how the Golden Rule and the story of the Good Samaritan come together to give us the Golden Rule of Compassion. Let's listen to Jesus tell the story in his own words:

> A man was going down from Jerusalem to Jericho, when he fell into the hands of robbers. They stripped him of his clothes, beat him and went away, leaving him half dead. A priest happened to be going down the same road, and when he saw the man, he passed by on the other side. So too, a Levite, when he came to the place and saw him, passed by on the other side. But a Samaritan, as he traveled, came where the man was; and when he saw him, he took pity on him. He went to him and bandaged his wounds, pouring on oil and wine. Then he put the man on his own donkey, took him to an inn and took care of him. The next day he took out two silver coins and gave them to the innkeeper. "Look after him," he said, "and when I return, I will reimburse you for any extra expense you may have" (Luke 10:30–36 NIV).

There are six actors in our story. There is the man who was beaten and robbed. There is the person who beat and robbed him. There are the priest and the Levite, whom we will call the preacher and the deacon, and there is the

Samaritan and the innkeeper, actors five and six. That's our cast.

The man beaten and robbed may have made a poor decision to travel the JJ highway when he did. Travelers were warned not to travel that road alone, definitely not at night. Possibly he did both and almost paid with his life for doing so. But let us not make the robber the victim of the man's poor decision. The man beaten and robbed is the victim.

As the sun comes up traffic picks up on the JJ highway. First the preacher comes walking, no doubt headed towards Jerusalem. He's thinking about his sermon and the demands of the day. He is also on the lookout for any sign of danger. Speaking of which, he sees the man. For whatever reason, fearing it could be a trap or perhaps just not wanting to get involved or having more important things to do, he crosses the road and walks on. Next comes the deacon who does the exact same thing. The man who was half-dead is now closer to three-quarters dead!

In walks the Samaritan, a despised foreigner. The Jews and the Samaritans did not care much for each other. *Gee*, thinks the Samaritan, *if the preacher and the deacon would not stop to help one of their own, what chance would I have of getting help if this is a trick and I get mugged?* Nevertheless, the Samaritan does stop. He does not see the man as a member of the majority, only as someone who desperately needs help. He bandages his wounds, puts him on his donkey, and takes him to a nearby inn. Actor number six walks in, the innkeeper. The Samaritan gives the innkeeper money for room and board and care of the man until he returns. If it costs more, he will pay it when he comes back!

Let's stop for just a few moments and ask the question, "Why did the preacher and deacon not stop to help the man, but the Samaritan did?" Jesus said the Samaritan was "moved with compassion." Then why was *he* moved with compassion and not the other two? We have defined compassion and have seen how it works, but we see in this story and know from our observations that some people seem more compassionate than others. Is compassion genetic? Is it something that has to be learned? Can it be learned? Is it something only possessed by "right-brained people," those who are demonstrative, affectionate, and "in touch" with their feelings?

To me compassion is not a feeling, it is an experience. It arises out of people relating to what another is going through. The true test for compassion is not just a "gut wrenching" experience, remember that is only one-half of the definition of compassion. The other half is we are compelled to take action to stop or alleviate the suffering of another. I have seen compassion expressed by persons who, on the surface, seem to be uncaring, yet they help others. So then how does it work? Why the Samaritan and not the other two? Why did Jesus use this foreigner? Was it more than just attacking the racism of his day and telling his listeners that God does not respect man-made boundaries? I think the Samaritan was moved with compassion because he related to the man. He knew what it was like to be down and out. He also knew what it was like to be passed by. He was not waiting for that day when he could get even. No, he lived by the Golden Rule, and on that day "he did unto that man what he wished others would have done to him!"

Now, the end of the story is the beginning of our Golden Rule of Compassion. There are two very important lessons we can learn from the story when we seek to help someone in need. These lessons are found in the answer to this question: What are the two most crucial parts in this story? The first is obvious. It comes at that wonderful moment when the Samaritan has that "gut wrenching" experience, is moved with compassion, and takes action to alleviate his suffering.

The second is after the story ends. It occurs when it's time for the injured man to leave the inn. We assume he did, don't we? Well, maybe we shouldn't! There exists the danger that he overstays his visit or worse yet becomes a permanent resident of the inn. How so? Here we have the potential for the classic case of codependency, which happens all too often when we help someone. How could it happen?

The Samaritan begins to like the feeling of being needed. He likes the endless words of gratitude showered on him by the man he helped, and the praise of others for being the man who did this wonderful thing. The injured man likes being taken care of and feeling special. Staying at the inn isn't so bad and, besides, the world outside can be a dangerous place. As for the innkeeper, he likes the arrangement. He always has a room occupied and appreciates the steady income. If the Samaritan brings in another victim of the JJ Highway, that's okay by him.

This is not the way the story was supposed to end, but that is the way it can and often does happen in real life when we seek to help those in need. Jesus would never have ended His story this way, nor does He want us to end the stories of those we help this way either. Jesus came to break the chains of dependence and He wants the same for our lives and the lives of those we would help. But the danger always exists and we run the risk of enabling people to stay in the inn if we are not careful. We must live by the Golden Rule of Compassion: Do unto others *only* what they cannot do for themselves.

Chapter Seven

"Sweet Pea"

Carl Payton, affectionately called "Sweet Pea" by his family and many friends, was a beautiful human being. He was loved and respected by all who knew him. Soaking wet, Carl weighed no more than 125 pounds and stood perhaps five feet, six inches tall. Small in stature, he was tall in the things which determine a person's size—integrity, honesty, trustworthiness, a strong work ethic, and a deep compassion for others. As an African-American growing up during the 1930s and 1940s, he knew the hurt and sting of prejudice; yet it did not make him bitter or cause him to judge certain people because of what others did to him. I was privileged to know Carl, call him friend, and work with him—he was the church custodian.

At the conclusion of Sunday worship there was always a long line of people waiting to see me. They all had their tragic tales and compelling reasons why I should give them money. We had safeguards in place, such as only paying rent money directly to the landlord. We also kept food in the church's refrigerator to give someone a sandwich. We also kept a tab at the local restaurant and gas station. Most, however, presented me with situations I had to respond to immediately; such as, they were being evicted the next day. I was pretty good at spotting the con artists, but with all my experience, it was sometimes difficult knowing who to believe.

A bigger concern to me was that even if this person were telling the truth, would I be helping her perpetuate the myth that money was the cause of all problems and the answer to all needs. Was I enabling her to leave or stay at the inn? Was I helping her identify and do something about her real problem, or was I helping her continue this dependent lifestyle?

The Bible says there are many reasons people are poor. Some are poor because they are lazy: "An idle person will suffer hunger" (Prov. 19:15 RSV). Others do not want to discipline their lives: "Poverty and disgrace comes to him who ignores instruction" (Prov. 13:18 RSV). Many make bad decisions: ". . . he who follows worthless pursuits will have plenty of poverty" (Prov. 28:19 RSV).

So there I stood talking with people who were living on the edge, possibly caused by laziness, lack of discipline, bad decisions, or a combination of all the above; or who were really in need through no fault of their own. My tendency was to err on the side of generosity and give them the money; that is, until one Sunday I saw Carl standing in the corner of the foyer, positioned directly over the shoulder of the person asking for help. It didn't take me long to discover that when Carl rolled his eyes, shook his head side to side, and then looked down, he was telling me not to give this person any money because he didn't need it. If he pressed his lips firmly together and shook his head up and down, then I knew the person really needed the help and would use the money for good purposes. I always followed Carl's unasked for, but greatly appreciated, advice.

Where did Carl get all this wisdom? These were Carl's neighbors. They shopped at the same stores, went to the same barbershop and beauty salons, waited together at the same clinic, and had their prescriptions filled at the same pharmacy. Carl's evaluation of their needs was not determined in a fifteen-minute conversation on Sunday, but by daily observations. Throughout Carl's life and even when he was dying of cancer, he did not want others doing for him what he could do himself, nor did he want people feeling sorry for him. He never wanted to stay in that inn one day longer than necessary. He expected the same of his neighbors, many of whom stood in those Sunday lines.

Carl was a very compassionate man and would give a neighbor the proverbial shirt off his back. Carl's compassion, however, was discerning. He extended it to those truly in need in a way which would help them solve their own problems and not make them dependent upon the giver. I loved and appreciated Carl as a person and learned a lot as his student. He helped me see the Golden Rule of Compassion in action.

I loved the people, the church, and the inner-city community, and I planned on staying there the rest of my life. God, however, had other plans.

Chapter Eight

The First Vision: A Great Expanse of Water

It is interesting how events take place of which we are unaware, and which seem so unrelated to our lives, only to discover in hindsight they were related and, indeed, integral to events yet to happen. Such were the events taking place not too far from my inner-city church in the late 1970s.

A large corporation wanting to expand its downtown headquarters approached an African-American church with a generous sum of money for their church building. In turn, this church approached another church with an equally generous offer for their church building. This church then, facing a declining and aging congregation, and realizing that they were not effectively ministering to their predominantly African-American community, accepted the offer. The church had talented and wealthy members; however, like a majority of inner-city churches, their members were getting older and lived in the suburbs.

The door of opportunity opened and they went through it, relocating in one of the fastest growing areas of the city.

Having gained a reputation for loving and knowing the inner city, several of the leaders of that church contacted me for my viewpoint on this opportunity of leaving the inner city for the suburbs. During the '60s and '70s, white churches were criticized for leaving the inner city. The church was sensitive to this criticism and didn't want to be perceived as "selling out."

I told them that I saw this to be a perfect fit. The African-American church would be better motivated and equipped to minister in their community. If they turned down the offer, they would be destined to a very slow death by attrition; this way, they could have new life in the suburbs. With the leadership and resources they still possessed, I could see no reason to believe they would be anything but successful. When word got out that the church was moving and that they were looking for a replacement for their retiring pastor, a colleague said to me, "Man, that will certainly be a plum church for some pastor!" *A sour one*, I thought to myself. *Who would want to live in the suburbs? Not me!*

One evening I received a call from a member of the church's pastoral search committee. I had been recommended for the position. He called to ask me to submit my résumé. Knowing that it would never go anywhere, I did. Several weeks later two visitors appeared at the morning worship. Seeing them, I knew I had made it past the first cut. I felt a sense of affirmation because our work in the inner city was being recognized. At the same time, a feeling of dread came over me when I considered where this might lead. A month or so later, they contacted me and said they wanted me to preach before the congregation, the final step before a church issues a call.

Suburbia! Following another outstanding pastor whose ghost would hang around like Dr. Cowley's; leaving the only church and community I knew; meeting the ambitious church-growth expectations of their leadership (who wanted a quick affirmation of their decision to relocate); rethinking ministry in terms of people who drive BMWs and have manicured lawns instead of people who take the bus and sit on stoops; leaving a people I loved and a church that had grown to be a leader among small inner-city churches, I said I would give them an answer in a week.

The night before the deadline, I literally stayed up all night seeking a sign from God. Throughout the night, Mickey would come to the top of the stairs and whisper, "Anything yet?"

"No," was my reply.

At 5:00 A.M. I crawled into bed. If God had given a sign, I missed it. For my career, this would have been "movin' up to the east side with a deluxe apartment in the sky," as *The Jeffersons'* sitcom theme song put it. It would be more money with a prestigious position. In my view, however, I already had the most prestigious job—I was the pastor of the Walnut Hills Baptist Church.

I turned the position down and rededicated myself to inner-city ministry. I ran into the retiring pastor of the other church a few months later. "They still really want you," he said.

"No," I said. "I've moved on to other things."

Three months later I received an invitation to have lunch with two members of the committee whom I knew personally. I tried to beg out of it, but they insisted. At lunch they made their case and asked me to reconsider. I told them I would get back with them on Monday with a final answer. It was Thursday. Leaving the restaurant, the feeling of dread became intense. For the first time, I began to seriously entertain the distinct possibility that I might say, "yes," and leave the inner city. This time there were no all-night vigils. I asked God to give me a sign that even *I* could recognize.

That Sunday, Connie, a member of my congregation, came to see me before the morning worship service. She wanted my advice. Connie was offered a new position that would mean a promotion with a substantial pay increase. It would involve additional responsibility, but would give her the opportunity to use more of her talents. The problem was that she was already in a very comfortable position. Everything was going great and she had made many close friends whom she didn't want to leave. What should she do? At that very moment I knew the advice I would give her would be the advice the Lord was giving me. I wanted to say, "Stay, Connie," but I couldn't. "Take the position, Connie," I said. "It's a wonderful opportunity."

I told Mickey that I was going to accept the call; the church still had to vote on me, but if I accepted, it was a done deal. After Sunday services we went to Mickey's parents' home for lunch. Mickey sat with her mother and father on the porch; the children played in the yard; and I attempted to watch the ball game on television, but kept dozing off. Somewhere between being asleep and awake, I received my first vision from God.

In the vision I saw a great expanse of water separating two large land masses. I was alone on one side and on the other was a multitude of people too great to number. There were children with hallow eyes and extended abdomens; old people crippled and in pain; people of every nationality—poorly clothed, hungry, emaciated, and covered with sores. It was a terrible sight. Their arms extended out towards me, as did their pleas for mercy. *This is only a dream*, I thought. I tried to wake up but couldn't. As I turned away from this dreadful sight I heard a voice say, "Reach out and touch." I said, as did the apostle Peter on the Joppa rooftop, "Surely not" (Acts 10:14 NIV). I felt ashamed. Feeling the presence of God and His unconditional love I finally did reach out. There in the middle of the water which separated us, we touched. A feeling of peace came over me. My decision to go to this church would, in some way, enable the poorest of the poor, the forgotten of the world to be helped. The next morning I told the search committee that I would accept their call. In a few weeks I was affirmed by the church at a congregational meeting. We did it! Now what?

The next twelve years were "the best of times and the worst of times." Some of my former parishioners said I had sold out, even though they didn't blame me. One of my inner-city pastor friends would not even speak to me. I would quickly discover that many of my new parishioners knew in their minds moving the church was necessary, but in their hearts they weren't so sure. There was still a lot of emotional attachment to the old church building. Many of the widows still lived in the old community. A few of my new parishioners hadn't made up their minds about me, or I about them. Some early decisions I made were not met with the approval of a few, and this would lead to a twelve-year standoff between us.

In spite of it all, the church was blessed with phenomenal growth. The budget was constantly over subscribed and the membership rolls increased dramatically, as did the Sunday morning attendance. Our giving to foreign mission ranked near the top in our denomination. Many creative ministries were started. The church was blessed with many wonderful people with great dedication and leadership skills. I still missed the inner city, however, and felt like a pilgrim in a foreign land. After visiting my members in the inner-city hospitals, I would often drive the surrounding streets. Seeing the homeless, the poor, and mentally ill, I wondered if I had heard God correctly. I was beginning to feel more comfortable in the suburbs and dispelled stereotypes I had about suburbanites. They were not born with a silver spoon in their mouths. They were successful because of hard work. True, they had an edge. They grew up in homes that valued education, maintained healthy diets, and were exposed to much more than inner-city kids. And while people are people and problems are the same wherever, suburbia folks had the means to fix theirs. I also discovered that suburban people, especially in my church, truly cared about the plight of the poor and were generous with their time and money.

The church was now one of the leadership churches in our denomination. Our children were in a good school system. They lived in a nice home and were growing up in a safe environment. The price of success, however, was twelve-hour days with little time off. And that vision I had, now ten years old, was becoming a faded memory. I concluded that it was just a psychological trick I played on myself so I would take the job.

Chapter Nine

The Phone Call

Dr. Jim Fidler is a compassionate man and a gifted surgeon. As the unofficial "doc" of the church, people go to him with their aches and pains. He always responds with patience and concern. He takes his Christian pilgrimage seriously. He often comes directly from all-night surgery to teach his young adult class on Sunday mornings. Jim is truly an exceptional human being and is dearly loved and admired.

One day Jim telephoned me to solicit help. A mission organization was bringing a Nicaraguan pediatrician and his wife to Cincinnati. A cancerous tumor was removed from his throat, but further treatment was needed. If Mickey and I would put up the couple in our home, Jim would see to his medical care. A few days later two very bewildered-looking people, Axel and Sherly Sobalvarro, stood at our front door. Sherly spoke some English; Axel, none. After showing them to their room, we sat down to dinner.

In the beginning things were awkward. It wasn't until Aaron began complaining about eating his broccoli that Sherly commented on the fact that her children, Axelito, nine, and Maria Jose, three, didn't like their vegetables, either. Axel then motioned for more mashed potatoes. He proceeded to deposit a very large glob of them on his plate. Sherly's eyes got big and she said, "That's a lot." Everyone started laughing. At that moment we became family. Axel and Sherly not only moved into our home but also into our hearts.

Axel was a much-loved and respected doctor in Nicaragua. Sherly headed up a fertilizer company which was nationalized when the Sandinistas came to power. When the dictator, Samosa, had been overthrown, they didn't flee Nicaragua as many did. They also managed to stay politically neutral and provided, under the circumstances, a reasonable standard of living for their family. After three months in Cincinnati, they thought it best that Sherly go home. They worried about their children and were afraid Sherly might lose her job.

They had to do what so many in countries other than America have to do—separate and live apart for the greater good of the family. It was a difficult time saying good-byes at the airport. Axel worried about his family's safety in war-torn Nicaragua and Sherly worried about Axel in a foreign land undergoing risky treatment for a life-threatening disease.

Weeks later, as I waited for Axel at the hospital, I bumped into Jim. I asked him, for the first time, about a prognosis. He told me that Axel had a nasty and progressive form of cancer. His only hope was massive amounts of chemotherapy and numerous radiation treatments and, of course, prayer. Additional surgery was ruled out. The treatments would make it impossible for Axel to salivate. A thermos of water was Axel's constant companion for several years.

The day finally arrived for Axel to go home. The doctors were pleased with his response to treatment. He would need to come back in six months for a follow-up visit. After hugs and goodbyes, Axel headed down the ramp to board his plane. He stopped, looked back, and said with a heavy accent, "Please come to Nicaragua. Mi casa es su casa." (My home is your home.) He then walked out of our sight.

A few weeks later my phone rang. The man who headed up the mission organization that arranged for Axel to come to the U.S. was taking a group of doctors to Nicaragua. Did I want to go? After talking it over with Mickey, I accepted. A local television station heard about the trip and sent reporters to interview us. Nicaragua was still very much in the news. Democratic elections were underway. The Sandinistas and Contras had signed a peace treaty. Former President Jimmy Carter and hundreds of United Nations observers were on hand to make sure the election would be properly carried out. There was still fighting going on in the mountains. The Sandinistas were still in control and no one was sure how they would respond if they were voted out.

That night we gathered around the television to see the interview. The coverage began with the words, "A group of Cincinnati doctors are traveling to war-torn Nicaragua." It then showed old file footage of helicopters firing rockets and wounded soldiers being carried out of the jungles. The narrator went on to talk about the hostility of the Nicaraguans towards the United States because of the economic embargo and the entire "Iran Contra" affair that was allegedly funneling huge amounts of money to the Contras. The coverage was sensational, exaggerated, and touched little on why we were going. By the time it ended my family was huddled tightly around me. Aaron looked up and expressed everyone's feelings; "Daddy you aren't going there?"

"I'll be all right," I said reassuringly. "It's nothing like that," . . . *or is it?* I thought to myself. The next evening we were on our way to "war-torn" Nicaragua.

Stephen Kinzer, a *Times* reporter, begins his book *Blood of Brothers* with these words, "Nicaragua's history is an epic of tyranny and rebellion." And so it is. Wholesale slaughter, enslavement, and plunder of Nicaragua began in the sixteenth century at the hands of the infamous Spanish governor Pedrarias. In 1821, the Central American countries won their independence from Spain and formed the United Provinces of Central America. That was short lived. In 1838, the independent Republic of Nicaragua was born. Nicaragua's exploitation continued into the twentieth century.

After independence was declared, the Conservative and Liberal Parties were formed and began a fierce struggle for power that ended in a bloody civil war. As incredible as it may be, on July 11, 1856, the one who emerged as president was an American named William Walker. His presidency and life were short lived. The Conservative Party ruled for the next forty years until the presidency of José Santos Zelaya at the turn of the century. Nicaragua greatly prospered during his six-year presidency. Pressured by President

William Howard Taft because of his opposition to U.S. businesses, Zelaya resigned and went into exile. U.S. troops were sent to Nicaragua to dispose of Zelaya's predecessor, the defiant Benjamin Zeledón. At Zeledón's funeral was a small man who wore a large hat—Augusto César Sandino. He would go on to lead a six-year guerrilla war against America.

There was a rise of sentiment against the United States' policy towards Nicaragua. America was also dealing now with the Great Depression. President Herbert Hoover called home U.S. troops in 1932. Sandino became a national hero; the little man took on the giant U.S. and won. He traveled to Managua where he and President Juan Bautista Sacasa agreed on February 2, 1933, on a peace treaty and the plans for the unification of Nicaragua.

Lurking in the shadows was General Anastasio Somoza Gracia, director of the National Guard. Somoza immediately began to consolidate his power and waited for the opportunity to make his move. A year after the famous meeting between Sandino and President Baututa, Somoza had Sandino assassinated. He then became president and began the dictatorship of the Somoza family which lasted for almost half a century.

Nicaragua was called the "rose garden" of Central America. The country basically worked under Somoza's rule and he provided a reasonable standard of living for the people. However, Somoza did not tolerate criticism and was brutal in dealing with those who did. The resistance movement began, taking on the name of National Liberation Front of Nicaragua, and the rebels called themselves the Sandinistas. When the popular newspaper publisher Pedro Joaquin Chamorro was assassinated by Somoza, the country rose up against the dictator. A twenty-year period of bloody warfare began in which thousands would die and hundreds of thousands would flee Nicaragua. In July of 1979, the Sandinistas took control of the country.

The Sandinistas were well trained in guerrilla warfare and knew how to bring down a government; they had little knowledge or experience, however, in running one. They tried to help the poor but their Marxist economic system was doomed from the beginning. There were also abuses of power. Stephen Kinzer noted, while living in Nicaragua during this time, that the only difference he saw between the Sandinistas and Somoza was that now the Sandinistas were the ones driving around in the white Mercedes. They also underestimated the importance of the Catholic Church. The people would never forgive them for the humiliating way they treated the Pope when he visited Nicaragua.

The U.S. was concerned about another marxist country so close to the U.S. border and the spread of this ideology into other Central American countries. The Nicaraguans who took up arms against the Sandinistas became known as the Contras (in Spanish, "against"). They were heavily supported and financed by the Ronald Regan presidency.

With the fall of Communism, the devastating U.S. embargo, the war weariness of the Nicaraguan people, their country in economic ruins, failed Sandinistan policies, and pressure from the international community, the Sandinistas agreed to hold an election. Daniel Ortega, a leading Sandinista, would run against Violeta Chamorro, the wife of the slain newspaper publisher.

922 Morris Street, Cincinnati, Ohio was home for the first eighteen years of my life. Through the good deeds of my parents, I witnessed compassion in action.

Walnut Hills Baptist Church: The place where I was baptized, married Mickey, was ordained, served for twelve years as pastor, and where I learned the Golden Rule of Compassion.

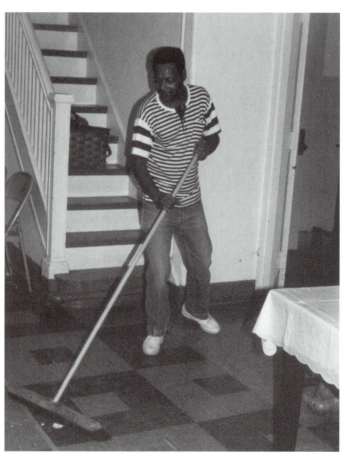

"Sweet Pea," the man who taught me
the Golden Rule of Compassion.

Axel and Sherly Sobalvarro at the
Matthew 25: Ministries' warehouse in Managua, Nicaragua.
Their visit to our Cincinnati home set in motion a series of events
which would bring about Matthew 25: Ministries.

When we began, the teachers in Nicaragua received only
two pencils and twenty sheets of paper each year.
The children received no supplies. We've shipped over
twenty-five million pencils and now make our own notebooks.

*"Please take our picture
so all can see the conditions
in our country,"
said this father holding his
severely burned baby
outside the emergency room
at the Velez Paiz Hospital.*

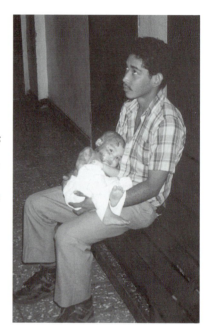

*Thirty United States Air Force airlifts . . .
thirty million pounds of humanitarian supplies . . .
1,250 forty-foot ocean-going containers . . .
and it all began with that one suitcase filled with supplies.*

Our first United States Air Force cargo plane, a C-130, at Sandino International Airport, Managua, Nicaragua.

Our first C-5 United States Air Force cargo plane. It can hold seven times the cargo of the C-130. It emptied our warehouse in Cincinnati and kept the dream alive.

*Lieutenant Colonel Karl McGregor (left) and I at
Andrews Air Force Base, Maryland. Karl was in the "driver's seat"
of a C-5 cargo plane during an airlift to Nicaragua and played
a crucial role in the early success of Matthew 25: Ministries.*

*The first group of men I picked up off of the
street corner in Walnut Hills to help us unload supplies.*

*I have always felt I did my best preaching
on a forklift, not in the pulpit.*

"What is a container?" I am often asked. Here it is.
It is a forty-foot truck which can carry thirty-eight of our
four-foot-cubed pallets, or up to forty thousand pounds of goods.
We've shipped 1,250 of them all over the world.

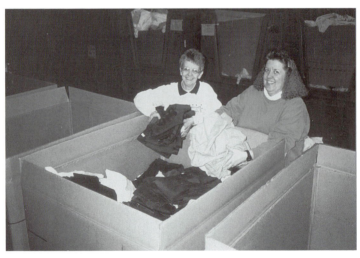

Anita Bowman (left) "runs" the warehouse and dishes out
generous portions of TLC to our volunteers. Patty Dilg (right),
my first staff person, is now director of operations.

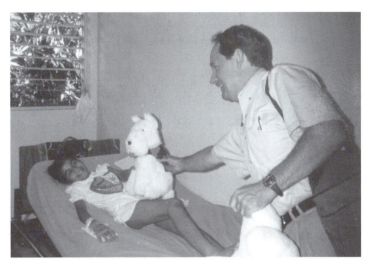

We arrived at the burn unit at the Velez Paiz Hospital, Managua,
Nicaragua, with beds, sheets, bandages, medicine,
air conditioners, paint, and gifts for the children.
The children especially liked the toys.

I had the honor of meeting a Las Flores, Nicaragua, family
who will soon be the recipients of a new home
built by Matthew: 25 Ministries.

A painfully typical scene in third-world countries.
Poverty is a cruel master. This photo was taken in Managua,
Nicaragua, next to a school we were rebuilding.

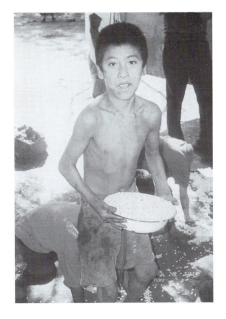

Distributing food can sometimes be messy. Yet not one grain of rice which spilled from the bag is left on the dirty ground.

Malnutrition takes a child's life worldwide every few seconds.

This picture was taken in Las Flores, Nicaragua.

Norma Hanna, a woman who left a very comfortable life in the U.S. to return to live in and help the people of Paso Real, the place of her birth. In this remote village, working with the courageous Norma, we have built a warehouse, a feeding center, and a multipurpose center. Our efforts have revitalized over fifteen villages. I have been blessed to know and work with her.

Too tired even to play. Life is difficult in third-world countries, especially for the children. This picture was taken in Nicaragua.

Matthew 25: Ministries has shipped over three million yards of fabric to hundreds of sewing centers in five different countries.

Here, my wife, Mickey, helps a little friend at the Fabreto orphanage, Nicaragua, model one of the garments made from the donated fabric.

Matthew 25: Ministries follows the wars. Here, children in Afghanistan received supplies shortly after war began. Photo courtesy of Bill O'Neal.

Matthew 25: Ministries is committed to helping children in the United States as well as abroad. These children in Appalachia show off their notebooks manufactured at the Matthew 25: Ministries print shop.

Alvaro Pereira (center), executive director of the American Nicaraguan Foundation, discusses plans for a new vocational center with Alfredo Cano (right), president of our village committee, and me. Alvaro and his family had to flee Nicaragua during the war, but returned with no malice to help thousands of his fellow Nicaraguans. He is a blessing to both them and me.

Students at the schools in Cape Town, South Africa, celebrate the arrival of a container of school supplies from Matthew 25: Ministries.

I've been blessed with having over 250 people accompany me to Nicaragua. Here are some of them. Back row (left to right): Bill Meyer, Dick Dostal, Dan Bloomfield, Aaron Mettey, Tim Mettey, and Michael Iery. Second Row: Mary Dostal, Sherly Sobalvarro, Father Guiermo, Esaf Meyer, Sandy Bloomfield, Patty Dilg, and Clare Mettey Iery. Kneeling: Alvaro Pereira, Mickey Mettey, me, and Heather Hopewell.

At Sandino International Airport in Managua, Nicaragua, Esaf Meyer poses with the United States Air Force Reserves crew from the 433rd Wing at Kelly Air Force Base, Texas. Esaf and her husband, Bill, have followed me to Nicaragua more than anyone else. Their love for the poor is only exceeded by their generosity.

*The 2003 Jefferson Award and the
2003 Jacqueline Kennedy Onassis Award medals
presented to Mickey and me at the Kennedy Center,
Washington, D.C., June 2003.*

*Matthew 25: Ministries headquarters, Loveland, Ohio.
They said we couldn't build it, but we did,
with our own hands and a lot of help from God.*

Chapter Ten

"When I Was Sick . . ."

When our group arrived at the ticket counter in the Miami Florida International Airport we were told, to our disbelief, that we could not board the plane for Nicaragua because we did not have visas. It didn't matter what the literature said—no visa, no ticket! "Where do you get a visa?" we asked. "In Nicaragua," they answered. "Well, how do we get a visa if we can't fly to Nicaragua?" They just shrugged their shoulders, *"lo siento"*—"I am sorry!" *Great. Now what are we to do?* A huge catch-22 and it would seem we were going to be cooling our heels in Miami. The possibility existed that this was as far south as we were going.

Suddenly an airline employee frantically waving his arms came running towards us. Everything had been taken care of; we could board the plane but we had to hurry. We knew that we had better get used to this because this was the way things were in Nicaragua.

We were no sooner airborne than the captain announced that the island below was Cuba. Cuba—the Bay of Pigs, Havana, Cuban cigars, Fidel Castro. Such a small piece of real estate and to think it was the center of a nuclear showdown that could have destroyed the world. Next, our plane set its sights on Managua and we flew over the beautiful blue Gulf of Mexico. The water stretched from horizon to horizon. *A huge expanse of water*, I thought as I recalled the vision of ten years before. In two hours we would be in Nicaragua. Remembering the vision, I was apprehensive about what I would find. Finally we broke through the clouds and got our first glimpse of Nicaragua. My heart pounded with excitement; soon I would set my feet on this exotic land.

Managua is situated on a flat, brown-and-green-checked plain. At its side is Lake Managua, the unfortunate benefactor of Managua's raw sewage. The lake is surrounded by several of Nicaragua's dozen or so volcanoes, ten of which are active.

On the ground we immediately saw the signs of the war. Anti-aircraft emplacements surrounded the airport. Old, rusted-out helicopters and armored personnel carriers were piled in scrap heaps everywhere. Once off of the plane, we were greeted by soldiers wearing oversized military uniforms, carrying big guns. Every move we made was carefully monitored. Taking photos at the airport was strictly forbidden. Even though the war was unofficially over, the airport was still militarily sensitive, especially to foreigners. We were looked upon with a great deal of suspicion.

A large group, including Axel and Sherly, were there to greet us. It was great seeing them again. We were so caught up in the excitement and newness of everything that we didn't notice that people in green uniforms were surrounding us. Our hosts huddled with two military officers—it was the visa thing again. We could not leave the airport without visas, so our hosts left to get the necessary paperwork. We were left alone with soldiers who carried big guns; that set in motion a series of scary events.

No one in our group spoke Spanish and no one carrying guns spoke English. They finally communicated to us that they wanted us to go across the street to the airport hotel. "No, we want to stay here. Our hosts will be back shortly!" They insisted and, since they had the guns, we went to the hotel. Once there, they told us we had to check into the hotel. Again, "We don't want to. We are not going to stay here." The guns prevailed, so we checked in as young men in starched, white uniforms carried our bags to our rooms. They then said they wanted to feed us. Now we understood, *this was going to be our last meal before they shot us!* We said we weren't hungry. They insisted; we ate.

While enjoying one of the most lavish meals we would experience on the trip, a young, thoroughly indoctrinated Sandinista officer who was fluent in English joined us. After he got all of the revolutionary rhetoric out of his system, we began talking human being to human being. We asked him about what had happened. "Why the airport hotel?"

"Well, because it is air conditioned and the airport is too hot for you to wait."

Okay. "What about checking into the room?"

"Oh," he smiled, "it looks good on the Ministry of Tourism report."

"And the food?"

"They thought you were hungry."

How mistrusting people can be when they can't communicate. After we finished lunch, our hosts arrived with our visas. We thanked our military escorts and even gave a few hugs. We were finally on our way.

With all of my social work background and experience, I was not prepared for what I saw driving to Sherly and Axel's home. Besides the civil war, which had drained every ounce of energy from Nicaragua, a 1972 earthquake leveled Managua—killing ten thousand and causing countless more to be homeless. After the earthquake people threw together anything they could find for homes. The streets of Managua were lined with a never-ending row of shacks. Electricity was unreliable, going off throughout the day and night, sometimes for hours. Water service was unpredictable. In a city of a million there were no stores. People sold items on the street corners or in converted garages. The exchange rate was ten thousand cordobas to one U.S. dollar. Shopping was like going on a scavenger hunt just to find a dozen eggs or a loaf of bread. Nothing in the country worked. I had never seen such poverty in my life; it was unimaginable and deeply disturbing.

We met a woman who could not have surgery until she found her own sutures. We visited hospitals in which there were no mattresses, and of those that did, only 20 percent had sheets. Surgical gloves were washed and reused dozens of times. In a three-hundred-bed hospital, the laboratory consisted of one microscope. The pharmacy was a small cabinet which contained all the medicine. There were no antibiotics, pain medication, soap, surgical gowns . . . nothing! I even saw two men sharing the same bag of IV solution.

The last night we were there we ate at a lakeside restaurant in the historic city of Granada. I became a little too adventurous and ate something my better judgment said not to. At 3:00 A.M. the next morning, my better judgment said "I told you so!" I was sick. All I could keep down was warm soda. Sherly and Axel were concerned and wanted me to stay, but I wanted to get home. Somehow I made it on the plane. I rested my forehead against the airplane window. We took off into a clear sky. A setting sun silhouetted the volcanic horizon with a red glow. I no longer saw roads and rooftops, but the many faces of the people I had seen and met. I then had a sobering thought. I was ill just as I had seen so many ill in Nicaragua. I could leave, go to the U.S., and receive medical treatment; they could not. I prayed, *Oh Lord, you have made me one of the ill so I can identify with those who suffer with no hope. Help me to help the people of Nicaragua. I do not speak their language. They are many; I am only one. A great expanse of water separates us. Show me the way, oh Lord.* I sat back in my seat hoping that it was only something that I had eaten and that I would make it home to Mickey and the children.

Two things seemed certain: Daniel Ortega would win the election and I would never see Nicaragua again. I was wrong on both accounts.

Chapter Eleven

Are Not My People Worthy of This?

Whatever I picked up in Nicaragua hung around the old intestinal track for several weeks. I was once again trying to keep pace with a growing church and a young family. Nicaragua was constantly on my mind. It took me several months just to sort through the experiences I had, the people I met, and the life-destroying poverty I saw—and the nagging questions.

Even if I wanted to do something, where would I begin? Where would I find the time and resources to do anything significant? Far more capable people have tried but with limited or no success. What made me think I could succeed where they had failed?

Maybe this was intended to be a once-in-a-lifetime event, a learning experience to be used in another time or place. Each time I entertained that thought, I would be revisited by the vision I had ten years before. No, I was confident, this was more than just a one-time adventure.

God meant me for Nicaragua or someone else I could take there. But who or what or how? I remembered the old proverb: "The longest journey begins with the first step." I decided to take that step and let God lead the way.

While my undergraduate degree was in economics, it didn't take an economist or a military strategist to see that the devastating poverty which gripped Nicaragua was caused by war and natural disasters; and the solution, economics. The people had said a resounding "no" to more fighting by voting Daniel Ortega and the Sandinistas out of office. This, in turn, ended the U.S.-sanctioned economic embargo against Nicaragua. From my perspective, what the country needed now was for the international community to invest in Nicaragua and create jobs.

I approached several businessmen in my church and asked them if they would accompany me to Nicaragua. The date, exactly one year after my first trip. Axel had been back in Cincinnati for a checkup and agreed that taking business people there would be good. All the businessmen who agreed to go were a great deal more enthusiastic about going than their wives.

A few days before we left I found myself suffering from fatigue and generally not feeling well. As with all trips, especially the early ones, I always feel a keen sense of responsibility for those accompanying me. I concluded, "That's all it is. Too much work and worry." In a few days I'll be basking in the Nicaraguan sun and enjoying a most hospitable climate—definitely a prescription for feeling better. I was also looking forward to seeing Sherly and the children and other friends I had made during my first trip.

Three days before we were to leave I told Mickey that I was going to sleep in. "This isn't like you," she said, "I think I'll go in late." "No," I replied. I told her that this was just precautionary. She got the children off to school and reluctantly went to work. Before she left she brought in the phone and put it next to the bed.

An hour or so later I found myself needing to hold onto the bedroom furniture going to and from the bathroom. I felt dizzy and weak. This was more than worry and work. Back in bed, I experienced a fluttering sensation in my chest. I broke out in a sweat and the room began to spin. I telephoned Mickey and told her to come home. The next thing I remembered I was looking up at the bedroom ceiling. I felt my head and moved my arms and legs. Luckily, I did not hit anything tumbling unconscious out of bed. A few minutes later Mickey came home. We went to the emergency room—ironically, or perhaps providentially—to the same hospital that was treating Axel.

I received immediate attention. The symptoms of most concern to the doctors were the ones associated with my heart. I was still feeling like the proverbial "wet dishrag" and was told that I had a low-grade temperature. I told the doctors that I had a plane to catch in three days. They said that they would do their best considering the importance of the trip. Mickey stood next to the bed smiling reassuringly. Mickey and I started dating when we were fifteen; it was impossible to hide anything from one another. I could tell she was worried.

All of the initial tests were negative. They did discover, along with a low-grade fever, that my white blood cell count was elevated. They wanted to admit me, "Just precautionary," they said. "Admit me!" I complained. The itinerary for the trip wasn't finalized: people had to be contacted, supplies packed, and I needed to meet once again with those going to discuss last-minute details. Mickey and the doctors were not going to budge. Admitted I would be.

Mickey went to check me into the hospital and the doctor and nurses left for other patients. One of the nurses closed the curtain around my bed. I was all alone. All alone, that is, except for every conceivable state-of-the-art piece of medical equipment, the latest electronic gadgets mounted on the walls, and cabinets bulging with medical supplies. There in that ER cubicle I thought, *What if this was serious and what if this happened while I was in Nicaragua?* The Nicaraguan hospitals have state-of-the-art nothing! Nothing would be mounted on the walls nor would I be lying in the newest hospital bed. The cabinets would be bare and there would not be as much as an aspirin in the pharmacy. Fortunately for me this happened this side of going to Nicaragua. *How fortunate we are*, I thought, *to live in the United States. People in Nicaragua die because they do not have access to such medical care or products we can buy at our local pharmacy. How unfortunate to live in Nicaragua.*

Once again I thought God was enabling me to vicariously experience the pain and suffering of the ill in Nicaragua, with only one difference: the countries in which we lived. The same germs affect us all in the same way, but we all do not have access to the same treatment. God was taking me to Nicaragua by way of that emergency room. Lying there on that bed with its crisp, ironed linens and fluffy pillows, surrounded by all that equipment and supplies, I heard that "still, small voice" say, *Are not my people in Nicaragua worthy of this?* While we are all God's children, He has a special place in His heart for those who suffer.

Okay, Lord, I had the experience. I got the message. Now let's get this over with so I can catch that plane. I must have been a slow learner because the experience was not going to end anytime soon or the way I would have scripted it. By the time I went to my room, my condition had deteriorated. My fever began to spike, preceded by chills that caused my body to shake, and my teeth to chatter. The next day they checked out my heart and I had what seemed like gallons of blood taken for tests. Albums of photos were taken in X ray, and still nothing. The only symptoms I had were fatigue and a temperature that was beginning to spike dangerously high.

It was becoming evident that, unless I had a Lazarus-raising miracle, I was not going anywhere. I telephoned those going on the trip to find out what they wanted to do. I knew Axel and Sherly would take care of them. Also the airline tickets were non-refundable. Since they were all "fired up" to go, they decided to go without me. I talked with them about a few objectives I wanted to accomplish on the trip. They told me to concentrate on getting better, they could handle the trip. The day of the trip I followed them, in my mind, all the way to Nicaragua. I was terribly disappointed and wondered why God had kept me from going.

A telephone call to Sherly the next day confirmed that they had arrived safely and all was well. That could not be said of me. That night was the worst of my ten-day stay in the hospital and possibly the worst night of my adult life. My fever was still out of control and I was getting weaker. At 1:00 A.M. I was taken to X ray. (The person taking me could never adequately explain why I was going at that particular hour of the night.) The X-ray machine was acting up, so I sat in a wheelchair for over an hour. I was feeling so bad that I began reciting verses of the Bible just to get through the ordeal. Back in my room, I began hallucinating. To combat this, I focused my mind on a building project at home; by morning, I knew where every bolt and piece of lumber would go. I was never so glad to see a sunrise in my life. That night was pure hell.

My doctor came in early to see me. Sitting on my bed, he began a thorough review of my chart, occasionally asking me questions I had already answered dozens of times. He was fishing and I knew it. He put the chart down and shook his head. The fever and the white blood cell count indicated that I had an infection, but where? "Could the cystoscopic examination have anything to do with this?" I asked. "Cysto exam," he replied with a blank look on his face. I reminded him that he had referred me to a urologist because I had blood in my urine. A week before, I had undergone my second such examination in the past two years. As with the first procedure, nothing was found to explain the presence of blood in my urine. While it was uncommon, there were documented cases of athletes passing blood after a strenuous workout. Since this always occurred after I ran, the urologist concluded that was the cause. There were several theories about why this happens. I was told that there was no cause to be alarmed.

Could I have picked up an infection from this invasive procedure? The urologist was called in immediately. After an ultrasound I was diagnosed with prostatitis. My prostate was the size of an orange and filled with infection. I was given mega doses of antibiotic. Several days later my temperature was normal and I was discharged. I would be homebound for three weeks. The IV needle was left in my arm so I could give myself antibiotics intravenously. I was amazed at the toll this infection had taken on my body and the length of the recovery time.

I spent the days reading the cards and letters which poured in from my church family, and I followed the progress of Desert Storm on television. I asked my friends who had gone to Nicaragua to come to my house and give me details about the trip. They had much to tell. I asked them what we should do. Economically, the country was out of their reach as businessmen. They felt that the area needing immediate attention was health care. One tragic scene after another was related of things they saw while touring several hospitals.

"We need to begin somewhere," I said. "What hospital would be the best place to begin?" Unanimously they answered, "The Velez Paiz Maternity and Children's Hospital."

"Well, then," I replied, "that's where we will start."

Chapter Twelve

Matthew 25: Ministries is Born

When Axel returned to the U.S. for one of his checkups, I asked him if he knew anything about the Velez Paiz Hospital. He smiled and said that he was on the staff at that hospital. He kept morning hours at the hospital and went to his clinic in the afternoon. It was not uncommon, however, for parents to bring their sick children to Axel's home. When this happened, he would excuse himself from whatever he was doing and patiently examine the children waiting at his front gate. Many could only afford a few pennies; he would shake his head at the offer and say that it wasn't necessary. Axel is a compassionate and well-respected man in Nicaragua.

When Axel returned to Nicaragua, he asked the director of the hospital to send me a list of supplies the hospital needed. Within a few days I received a fax from Dr. Julio Florez listing the items urgently needed. I would later discover that such a list, regardless of the country, was always the same: soap, sutures, surgical gloves, linens, beds, mattresses, etc. We are all human beings on the same planet, with all the same needs. List in hand, I went to work acquiring the first humanitarian supplies Matthew 25: Ministries would send to the suffering of the world.

Money was quickly raised and the supplies were purchased. The supplies came to the church building where they were readied for shipment. Next was the issue of transportation. How do we get our supplies, all one ton of them (that seemed like a lot then), to Nicaragua? I contacted a commercial airline and was able to get a favorable rate of thirty-five cents per pound! We loaded the supplies on a pickup truck and took them to the airport—next stop Nicaragua.

I planned for the supplies to arrive during my second trip to Nicaragua. The country was in the beginning stages of its transition from a marxist regime to a democracy. There were still many unsettled issues and tensions between those in power and those who used to be. The country still lay in a state of economic ruin and most of the infrastructure was still unreliable. I wanted to visit the hospital myself and oversee the arrival of the supplies.

As soon as our plane touched down, I knew things were different. On my previous trip, the atmosphere at the Sandino Airport was threatening, and the only people present were military; this time, hundreds of people lined the balcony at the airport. Dressed in bright colors and waving handkerchiefs they shouted, *"Bienvenidos a Nicaragua."* "Welcome to Nicaragua!" *Surely these could not be the friends or family of the people on the plane*, I thought. There were not that many people on the plane. Later I learned that people just came to the airport to greet arriving planes. They came to the place that was their connection to the outside world which had been denied them for so long. They were so happy to be free. I will always remember getting off of that plane and seeing that mass of jubilant people; still as poor as the first trip, but now they were free. I would find a new sense of optimism in Nicaragua.

All the way to Nicaragua I hand-carried a microscope on my lap because I didn't want anything to happen to it. This was an item at the top of Dr. Florez's wish list. Upon arrival, I asked Axel and Sherly if the supplies had arrived. Sadly, they hadn't and would not arrive for another three months. I discovered on that trip that I needed to find another means of transporting supplies. Suitcases were too small and flying them aboard commercial airplanes was as uncertain as the Nicaragua economy.

While we failed in an attempt to get the supplies to Nicaragua during our visit, the trip was successful nevertheless. We traveled the country and met many people who would prove to be instrumental in our attempts to help Nicaragua. We also conducted an extensive tour of the Velez Paiz Hospital which had truly lived up to its infamous reputation.

Surgeons, in their street clothes, operated on patients in theirs. The hallways were filled with the sound of children crying. Medication was limited and given only to the children in greatest pain. There was no air conditioning or proper ventilation in most of the rooms. The children's salty perspiration ran into their wounds. Women slept two to a bed with their newborns hanging in baskets at the ends of the beds. Most of the hospital's windows had glass missing, allowing dust to blow in with regularity. Everything in the hospital needed painting, fixing, or replacing. *Dear God*, I prayed, *where do we start?!*

Later that morning, Axel and I came upon a man sitting patiently on a bench outside the ER. He was holding his infant son. The child was severely burned over most of his body. It was a terrible sight. A child in the U.S. would have been rushed into one of those ER cubicles with all its state-of-the-art equipment and cupboards full of medicine and supplies. An IV would have been started immediately. Once stabilized he would be transported to the burn unit of a hospital. There he would receive the best of care. Not so in Nicaragua. For three hours he waited his turn as other ill and injured children were seen by a dedicated yet overworked and inadequately supplied staff of doctors and nurses.

"Take their photograph," Axel said. "No, Axel. I can't." Axel asked the father's permission and told him who I was. The father agreed with Axel. "The world needs to know what it's like in Nicaragua," he said. I took his photograph and told him I would do my best to tell the world about Nicaragua. On successive trips, I inquired about the boy. No one could say how he was; there were so many.

Sixty five percent of Nicaragua's four million people were under the age of sixteen. Education was crucial to Nicaragua's future. We received an appointment with the minister of education. Again, more unbelievable stories. Each teacher received just two pencils and twenty sheets of notebook paper for the entire year. The children received absolutely no school supplies. The school buildings were in shambles, the textbooks were filled with revolutionary images, ideology, and mistrust. Elementary-age children carried their desks to and from school because the schools were not secured. One school we visited had eleven hundred students and only one bathroom—a wooden shed with a hole in the ground. And yet the children came to school each day and the teachers taught under impossible circumstances. I told the minister of education that I would find school supplies for Nicaragua. I didn't know how, but I would, some way.

As the song goes, "You are always on my mind." Well, for me it was, "Nicaragua was always on my mind." My sermons, Bible lessons, and personal conversations always seemed to come back to stories of Nicaragua and my experience there. I'm certain some were thinking, *enough already!* However, most people were genuinely concerned about the plight of the Nicaraguans and wanted to help. I formed a small committee and we began planning for another trip. A businessman allowed us to use thirty-five hundred square feet in his warehouse where we could receive and process medical supplies. I also learned about the Denton Amendment.

Jeremiah Denton was one of the longest held POWs of the Vietnam War. Following his return to the U.S., he rose to the rank of admiral in the United States Navy and was elected to the U.S. Congress as a senator from Alabama. While in Congress, he helped pass the Denton Amendment. Under this amendment the United States Air Force was permitted to carry on their cargo planes humanitarian aid from non-governmental, not-for-profit organizations at no cost to the organization. In the fall of 1991, we submitted our first application.

The next order of the day was becoming incorporated with the state of Ohio and submitting the documentation needed to become a federally recognized not-for-profit organization and receive that all-important designation of 501 (C) (3). Unless an organization receives this designation, contributions are not tax-deductible; thus, U.S. corporations will only donate supplies to 501 (C) (3) organizations.

Before we could file the necessary forms we needed a name and a written statement of purpose. We knew we were called by God to help the poor in Nicaragua, but how? And in what way? And the name? I only knew the word Nicaragua could not be in our name because Americans cannot pronounce it. It always comes out Nica-wa-wa! Ouch! What would we call ourselves?

Chapter Thirteen

Matthew 25:34–40

I grew up in a large stone inner-city house. Tucked away, all cozy inside, was a large, happy, secure family. I was the youngest of four children. I was a sickly and frail child and consequently received a lot of attention. A birth defect, ruptured appendix, septic hip, allergic reactions to food, and many other maladies raised serious questions about my chances of making it to puberty. I spent a great deal of time at Children's Hospital and on my mother's lap on our back porch. Little did I realize at the time that those back porch lap sessions were really Bible 101. To take my mind off of the two intruders in my young life, illness and pain, my mother told me the great stories of the Bible. Well read and versed in the Scriptures, she brought the stories and their characters to life with dramatic flare. David and Goliath was my favorite story. I imagined myself to be the little shepherd boy and my illnesses the great giant Goliath. I learned during those back porch lap sessions that no problem was bigger than a person and God. I outlived the worry of my early demise and would experience some of the happiest, carefree years of my life. My life was made up of my family, baseball, playing in Eden Park, and getting my way. Did I mention I was spoiled?

When I became fifteen my life would take a dramatic turn, setting in motion a life's journey I could never have imagined. Within several months that large people-filled home became a house of grief and loneliness for my mother and me. My grandmother, independent, strong and spirited, whose only beef with the Lord was that He didn't make her a boy so she could have done all those boy things, died suddenly of a heart attack. Gone was the only grandparent I ever really knew, whose love was unconditional and whose large, cushiony granny lap and large sagging arms were refuge from all of life's troubles.

Within months of her death, my father developed stomach cancer and died that autumn. He was a quiet, hard-working man who was always there for his family and friends. His stay in an orphanage due to the death of his mother and the fact that his father couldn't handle eleven children made Dad's family his first priority and the joy of his life. Botched back surgeries and the crude surgical instruments of his day caused him endless pain. However, I never did hear him complain. He was my hero.

When Dad died, my brothers and sister were married and starting families. Mom and I were living by ourselves in that big, now empty house. My mother was completely consumed with grief. Emotionally, she died with my father. We buried Mom nineteen years later. A few years after Dad died, I found myself living alone in a one-room apartment while attending the University of Cincinnati. All that sustained me during this time was my high-school sweetheart, Mickey; playing baseball; and my faith in God.

At first I hated living alone. I had grown up in a large, people-filled, noisy home. I was now living in a shoebox-size room in a building occupied by strangers. I came in late and left early. I spent as little time there as possible. A larger room down on the second floor became available and I took it. I was now living in a breadbox-size room. It did, however, have a large window with a nice view. I had been living alone now for about six months, and it was not all that bad. I discovered that being alone does not mean you have to be lonely. Being alone and without a television or telephone forced me at first, then allowed me, to take that inward journey.

I wrestled with issues of faith and worked through my own theology. I developed a deeper and closer relationship with God and fell deeply in love with His son, Jesus. As a graduate of the back porch lap Bible 101 school, I took all I had been taught, tweaked it somewhat, and made it my own. I also found myself looking forward to evenings, which not long ago I dreaded. I no longer listened for monsters lurking in the quiet, but listened instead with great anticipation for the still, small voice of a living God. It took time, but the quiet was no longer a painful reminder of what was once my life but was no more; it was now the sound of what could be. I began the habit of reading the Bible each evening with study aids, listening to Billy Graham, and a radio show called *Moon River*. I spent protracted periods in prayer on my knees beside my bed.

One night during prayer I had this overwhelming urge to raise my right hand. I reasoned that it was an inward desire to reach out to God. When I raised my hand and extended my arm I felt much love and acceptance. Then to my indescribable shock I felt someone physically grab my hand. The touch was both assuring and frightening. I jumped up and turned on the light. Someone was in my room. A quick check of the closet and under the bed confirmed that I was alone. I sat on the edge of the bed for most of the night. I couldn't sleep. I tried to make sense of what had happened. The scientific, rational, skeptical side of me reasoned that it was nothing more than a psychophysical response by my brain to my experience. Something happened that I wanted to happen to validate my experience. The other side of me said simply, *God touched you.* All I knew was that I felt something.

That night I developed a tremendous ache in my gut for the poor and a longing to rid them of the poverty which enslaved them. I kept hearing, *When I was hungry . . . when I was thirsty.* The next morning I paused by my window before leaving for class. I saw a man walking on the sidewalk. (I still don't know the significance of that man or what he represents, but the image of seeing him there has stayed with me.) I heard that still, small voice say, *Wendell, I want you to serve Me all day, every day.* Gradually, the experience that night came together for me in Matthew 25:34–40 when Jesus said:

> Then the King will say to those at his right hand, "Come, O blessed of my father, inherit the kingdom prepared for you from the foundation of the world; for I was hungry and

you gave me food, I was thirsty and you gave me drink, I was a stranger and you welcomed me, I was naked and you clothed me, I was sick and you visited me, I was in prison and you came to me." Then the righteous will answer him, "Lord, when did we see thee hungry and feed thee, or thirsty and give thee drink? And when did we see thee a stranger and welcome thee, or naked and clothe thee? And when did we see thee sick or in prison and visit thee?" And the King will answer them, "Truly, I say to you, as you did it to one of the least of these my brethren, you did it to me" (NIV).

While trying to come up with a name for our work in Nicaragua, I shared this twenty-year-old experience with a friend. He said, "Let's call our work Matthew 25: Ministries"—and so we did.

Chapter Fourteen

Our First Cargo Plane

January 16, 1992, was the date of the first Matthew 25: Ministries work group to go to Nicaragua. Twenty-two somewhat apprehensive-but-caring people went to Nicaragua for ten days. For most it would be the experience of their lives. They all had similar concerns. *Will I be able to eat the food and drink the water? What if I get sick? Will it be safe?* Their concerns were all short-lived. Within a matter of a few days everyone had acclimated themselves to Nicaragua and were captivated by the beauty and grace of the Nicaraguan people. No one, however, got accustomed to the poverty.

Our work project was the renovation of the emergency room at the Velez Paiz Maternity and Children's Hospital. We also oversaw the arrival and warehousing of our supplies which were scheduled to be airlifted to Nicaragua the week we were there. Months prior the supplies were carefully palletized in Cincinnati and trucked to Wright

Patterson Air Force Base (WPAFB) in Dayton, Ohio. There they were loaded aboard a C-130 USAF cargo plane and flown to Nicaragua. A C-130 cargo plane holds roughly a semi truckload of supplies. We thought at the time the C-130 was the largest airplane imaginable and its cargo truly a mountain of supplies. We would soon discover that God had much bigger plans.

Renovating the ER during the day with a constant stream of patients coming and going was not an easy task. We could not work at night because the electricity kept going off and the wattage was not sufficient for us to see. If the job was going to get done, it would have to be during the day. We would have to work around rooms full of people needing emergency care. At first the staff perceived us as one more obstacle to overcome. When they could see that we meant business and the ER was being transformed right before their eyes, they became more receptive and helpful. They had seen many people from other countries come, take pictures, and make speeches filled with empty promises, only to leave and never return. After several days they could see we were different.

The ER had not been painted in thirty years. Plaster was falling into the patients' beds. Doors were missing and the windows had rusted open or shut. There was no soap or disinfectants. It became apparent that sanitary supplies were going to be at the top of our "need list." We marveled daily at what the ER staff was able to do with the little they had. Medical people in our group were especially aware of this. If they had to work in this setting, they said, they would have to be completely retrained. They became big admirers of the staff in the ER. The Nicaraguan doctors and nurses did not need more training, they needed supplies. All of this placed an increased importance and urgency on getting humanitarian supplies to Nicaragua.

Even for those who worked in such settings back in the U.S., the things we observed daily in that ER were disturbing. Individuals in our group would often remove themselves to take a "timeout" to work through something they saw. On one particular day, we had to call time out and get the group together to talk and pray through one such incident. A little baby was brought into the ER. His lifeless, disease-ravaged body was placed on a bed by his mother, whose sobbing could be heard throughout the hospital. The staff heroically tried to save the little baby, but it was obvious he was beyond their means to save with the supplies and equipment they had. Their efforts were soon focused on consoling the grieving mother. Everyone stopped what they were doing. Some bowed their heads, other shook theirs in anger. A life was lost simply because of the country in which he was born.

To Nicaraguans, all Americans are rich. During those first few days the people stared at us in disbelief. They had never seen rich people down on all fours scrubbing floors. We were also a paradox. For years they had been told that Americans didn't like Nicaragua and were the main cause for their impoverished lives. But here we were, doing what was reserved for the lowest paid in their society. The Americans they had met in Nicaragua often had a political agenda and were anti-U.S. We did not fit into their American stereotype. We were simply there to help, wanting nothing in return. While the love of Jesus brought us there, we did not come to convert them to any religious doctrine or political view. We merely wanted to share with them the things we had, again motivated only by the love of Jesus and the compassion He placed in our hearts. By trip's end, everyone in the hospital was visiting the ER to see us work and observe the job of refurbishing. We became the recipients of gifts understood in any language, appreciated in any culture—hugs!

On Wednesday we were notified that the USAF plane carrying our supplies would land the next day at the Sandino Airport. We were given permission to go on the tarmac, watch the plane land, and greet the crew. The first time I stepped on that tarmac the military would not allow me to take a photograph. Now our entire group could go out and welcome the arrival of a U.S. military plane.

I thought we were on the old TV show *Fantasy Island* when someone in our group shouted, "The plane! The plane!" Sure enough, there it was. The biggest most beautiful plane I had ever seen. We walked out to greet and thank the crew, who would be the first of literally hundreds of crew members we would meet. Their conduct and all who followed them made us proud to be Americans. The plane was promptly offloaded and the supplies placed on several trucks. Following interviews with the local media, we were on our way to the hospital. Many were thinking of that little boy who had died and hoping that perhaps the next child might be saved because of the supplies in these trucks.

Chapter Fifteen

When We Get a "No," It's Because God Has a Bigger "Yes"

Twelve months later we were off again to Nicaragua; another work party and our second planeload of supplies. This time it was a C-141 cargo plane (which carries about two-and-a-half semi truckloads of supplies). Getting this plane was a story in itself. I'm still not certain who all the players were.

After Desert Storm, the Denton Program was in disarray. Applications were sent to Washington but no one was processing them or working with NGOs (non-governmental organizations) in locating planes to fly their cargo. One of the crucial objectives of this work party was the installation of twenty-five large air conditioners in the Velez Paiz Hospital. This would completely air condition the children's burn unit. We were within days of leaving for Nicaragua and still had no plane or prospects of finding one.

The first inauguration of Bill Clinton was about to take place. While I did not vote for him nor was invited to the ball, I began contacting everyone who was going to the inaugural. I pleaded with them to take a few minutes from their inaugural partying to find us someone who could order up a plane. I contacted over fifty individuals. The most any of them would commit to was, "I'll try." A few days later I received an urgent call from Washington saying we had one day to get our supplies to Wright Patterson Air Force Base. In five days the plane would be in Nicaragua. After the plane landed and the supplies were offloaded, I asked the pilot who authorized the flight. He shook his head and said, "You don't get any higher than this." He was referring to the White House. I knew it was a lot higher than that!

It was also on this trip that God said the same words He said to the prophet Isaiah, "Enlarge the place of your tent, stretch your tent curtain wide, do not hold back, lengthen your cords, strengthen your stakes" (Isa. 54:2).

I received a phone call at Sherly and Axel's home from the person who coordinated the military flights in and out of Nicaragua. He told me that our supplies were coming aboard a USAF C-5 cargo plane. They were with the supplies of several other relief organizations. I told him this was a mistake. He insisted he was right and asked me to be at the airport to claim my cargo.

I was confident that our supplies were not on this plane. I also expressed to Sherly my doubts about a C-5 being able to land. "The airport runway is not long enough," I said. As a precaution, Sherly and I went to the airport but decided not to take the mission team or any trucks.

After receiving permission, we walked through the guard station and onto the tarmac. I saw immediately that

I was wrong about one thing. There before us, in all of its splendor, was a USAF C-5 cargo plane. Apparently the runway was long enough. It was the first time I had seen a C-5 close up or watched supplies being offloaded. It was immense. The military attaché, whom I had spoken to on the phone, came over to apologize. Our supplies were not on this plane but would be flown in the next day aboard a C-141. I assured him his apology was not necessary. As I stood there I looked at this huge instrument of mercy and saw its enormous cargo bay. I looked up to God and said, *Lord, we've got to get one of those.* I felt like Moses standing on the mountaintop looking at the Promised Land. God was giving me a glimpse into the future.

Following that second work party and airlift it was becoming apparent to me that God was calling me away from my church and to a life devoted to caring for the poor. I would certainly miss the people of the church but not the politics.

Following that trip, I injured my back and would suffer through a year of painful and useless therapy, two spinal injections, and unsuccessful surgery. I was in such pain that I could hardly stand to preach. The day after my last sermon I had my second back surgery. A small bone fragment was pressing against my sciatic nerve. A competent surgeon who knew what to look for ended my year-long ordeal in a few minutes.

Convalescing at home provided me ample time to consider what I had done. For the first time since seminary, I did not have a congregation or a paycheck. If Matthew 25: Ministries was to become a C-5-cargo-plane-size effort, I would have to give it my complete attention and all my energy. Mickey and I decided that we would live on and finance the ministry with my severance pay from the church. Hopefully, before the money ran out, the ministry would be financially self-sufficient.

The warehouse that had been available to us and was rent-free was neither anymore. I found a five-thousand-square-foot warehouse and signed a year's lease, costing the ministry $900 a month. We now had our own empty warehouse, but had no idea how we would get supplies to Nicaragua if and when we got them. Mickey went back to work.

Soliciting supplies presented me with a steep learning curve. I began by going through Wal-Mart and finding the items we needed: pencils, notebooks, bandages, tape, and soap. I copied the names of the manufacturers and their phone numbers from the back of the packages and began calling. I discovered early on that the person you don't want to ask for is the person in charge of donations. They receive so many requests that they develop a polite but firm, "We already give all we can. Have a nice day!" I learned that sales reps, plant managers, and environmental people were the best to contact. They have the responsibility of disposing of what the industry calls, "distressed material"—absolute, damaged, excess inventory, and closeouts that are not good enough to sell, but a shame to throw away.

I located a sales rep from a pencil company. After telling him of the situation in Nicaragua and how the poor children have no pencils, he asked me how many pencils I needed. I told him that each teacher in Nicaragua receives only two pencils for the year.

Again he asked, "How many do you want?"

I thought, *I don't know how many. I don't want to be too low or too high.* I replied, "I think I might shock you."

"Go ahead," he said.

"Twenty thousand pencils."

"Reverend," he said, "you gotta think bigger. We make that many in a few minutes." He shipped me one quarter of a million!!!

It took us over a year, but we did it. We filled that warehouse. Fewer people, however, were coming to volunteer. Days would go by and I would be the only one there. I still had not solved the transportation problem nor had God revealed to me His plan or even if Matthew 25: Ministries was in His plans. Several churches inquired about my availability. They were leadership churches with challenges and comforts similar to my previous church. I turned them down and wondered to Mickey if I was doing the right thing. Our funds were running low and the ministry did not seem to be in God's immediate plans.

One day I received a call that I thought would be the death knell of Matthew 25: Ministries. It was the realty company; our lease was up and they had leased our space to a company that wanted immediate occupancy. We had fifteen days to vacate. It was over. The dream of reaching the poor of the world had come to an end. I began to think of ways of disposing of the supplies. Possibly there was another organization to which I could donate them. A few days later, I met a member of Matthew 25: Ministries' Board of Directors. Like the others, he seldom attended meetings and never helped at the warehouse. It wasn't that he didn't support the work; he had gotten on with other things. The initial passion and excitement were gone. I remember telling him that Matthew 25: Ministries was over. He was shocked, but didn't offer any help or solutions. That was certainly a low day in my life when I verbalized what I was thinking.

It just is not in my nature to quit. I believed that God was in this and wanted us to succeed. I also learned that when we receive a big "no," it's because God has a bigger "yes". If we get all we want the way and when we want it, we often miss bigger things and better ways. Life is made up of far more seeking than finding. Finding is only the beginning of more seeking.

I called WPAFB and talked with the sergeant. I told him that I had called U.S. senators, generals, and admirals, but no one knew anything about the Denton Program or how to arrange for a plane if they did. "Sergeant, do you know where I can get a plane?"

"Yeah," he said, "There's a captain in Texas who often calls up here looking for cargo for his Reserve flights."

That afternoon I contacted Capt. Karl McGregor. I did not know it at the time, but Karl would play a crucial role in our efforts to get supplies to Nicaragua. He also became a good friend and is certainly a friend of the "least of these." I told him the situation we were in and asked, "Captain, can you help us?"

"No problem," he said. "We can fly a mission in two weeks. Can you have cargo ready by then?"

"Captain," I said, "It's been ready for months."

Chapter Sixteen

Our First C-5 Cargo Plane

It had taken almost a year to collect a warehouse full of supplies and twelve months trying to find a plane. Now I had less than two weeks to get the supplies north fifty miles, to Wright Patterson Air Force Base. There the supplies would be readied for the C-5 cargo plane flying in from Kelly Air Force Base, Texas. I finally got the plane, now would I be able to pull it off? Previously, I had a large church to go to for help; now I was pretty much all alone.

With no money and no contacts in the trucking business, how was I going to get the supplies to the air base? How much could the plane hold? Did I have the supplies correctly placed and secured on the pallets? Once in Nicaragua, how many trucks would I need to transport the supplies to . . . to where? I didn't have a warehouse nor knew of anyone who did. What about customs, and all that paperwork Nicaragua is famous for? The two previous cargo planes were much smaller and I had others helping me.

I felt like the man who said to Jesus, "Lord, I believe, help me in my unbelief!" Butterflies the size of condors began flapping their wings in my stomach. I knew I could do it, but didn't have a clue how.

Two weeks later I was off to Nicaragua. The supplies were sitting in a hanger at WPAFB ready for their trip south the next day. I contacted the Nicaraguan government before leaving and talked with Margarita Caldera, secretary general of education for the Nicaraguan government, for the first time. Intelligent, bilingual, personable, and a tremendous administrator, she assured me that everything would be taken care of. Since most of the supplies were for the schools she would personally oversee their arrival, documentation, and distribution. Margarita would not only make this trip a successful endeavor, but many others to follow.

As my plane took off, I thought once again how things in life can change so quickly. A few weeks before I thought the dream was coming to an end. Now, miraculously, the Cincinnati warehouse sat empty, ready for its new tenant. I did not have to find another organization to take the supplies, or worse, truck them to the landfill. Soon the supplies would be helping thousands of impoverished children in my beloved Nicaragua.

Throughout this first difficult year of Matthew 25: Ministries, I can see now it was never just "I." It was always "We." God was always with me. It only seemed like "I" when my faith was weak. As the poem by Margaret Powers entitled "Footprints in the Sand" says, when I felt alone and abandoned, "and only saw one set of footprints in the sand, it was then God was carrying me." The dream would stay alive for one more airlift! God was not only carrying me, but also Matthew 25: Ministries and one big plane!

Axel and Sherly's smiling faces greeted me at the airport. After an evening of visiting with friends, I said, "*Buenas Noches.*" We had to be at the airport early the next day. The C-5 was scheduled to land at 11:00 A.M.; our day started at 6:00 A.M. We needed security clearance to enter the airport and the necessary paperwork to take possession of the supplies once off of the plane. This meant that we had to visit the Ministry of Education, Ministry of Health, Ministry of External Cooperation, Customs, and a few others. After receiving their stamps of approval, we went directly to the airport. It was 10:30 A.M.

The cloudless sky warned of a hot day ahead, especially standing on that black heat-radiating tarmac. Unlike the last plane, this time we had to go through several guard stations, each carefully checking our paperwork. We also could not wander around like a bunch of tourists. We had to wait in a small sectioned-off area. A nearby guard carrying a big gun made following the rules a good idea.

Finally, someone said excitedly, "Look, there it is!" All we could say was, "Oh, Dear God, it's enormous." There it was, flying directly overhead. It circled the airport and then leveled off for its approach. Within a few minutes it was on the ground. It made a textbook landing—one of many we would witness during the years ahead. Surrounded by baton-waving airport personnel, it taxied to our end of the airport.

I stood on the tarmac of the Sandino Airport watching that C-5 touch down. I looked up to God and said, *Well, Lord, we got one of those. I hope there's more!* I was assured there was.

Airport and embassy personnel walked out to the plane. No body or no thing was coming off of that plane until the correct protocol was observed and documentation was verified and okayed. When all of the above was accomplished, the flight crew received the go-ahead to begin the unloading. The plane's hydraulics lowered the body of the plane and raised its nose. There in its cargo bay were our precious supplies, covered with plastic and securely strapped down to thirty-five metal plane pallets. The Air Force did a great job of palletizing our supplies; not one item was missing or damaged.

Large airport forklifts began swarming around the plane. Compared to the size of the plane, they looked like tiny crabs swimming around a blue whale. One at a time the forklifts positioned themselves at the end of the plane. With their forks raised, they were ready to receive the cargo. Each plane pallet can weigh up to eight thousand pounds. Their weight is so evenly distributed that it takes only two airman to push a pallet off of the plane onto the waiting forklifts. Once the thirty-five plane pallets (carrying over 270 of our pallets) were offloaded, they were taken to another area for staging. There the plastic and strapping were removed. Customs personnel inspected the cargo and, after more paper signing, the supplies were ours.

The flight crew was efficient, professional, and a joy to work with. They wore their uniforms well and were wonderful ambassadors of the U.S. Little did I know then, but they would be the first of many C-5 crews with which I would have the privilege of working. They were fantastic and had that great "can-do" spirit. I was always proud of them and they made me proud to be an American.

Within four hours of touchdown we stood and waved to the crew as the plane took flight. Now our work began. We had to load the supplies onto waiting trucks and secure them in a warehouse loaned to us by the Ministry of Education. It was 2:00 P.M. We estimated that it would take another four hours. We soon discovered that Murphy's Law, which says if things are going to go wrong, they will at the worst possible time, was alive and well in Nicaragua.

The warehouse, which we saw for the first time the day before, was on the opposite side of Managua. The street outside the warehouse was alley size. The gravel-covered unloading area was on the side of the warehouse. There was room for only one truck at a time. It was agreed that it was best for the trucks to back in. There was a tolerance of no more than a foot on each side of the gate. Maneuvering each truck through the gate would take the skills and patience of the best drivers. The first truck arrived. Gravel flying, people whistling and screaming directions, and increasingly irritated drivers all gave me some indication that we had better reassess our schedule. It took the first truck thirty minutes in daylight to get through the gate. Night was soon upon us and we had another fifteen trucks waiting to offload. The first pallet was not in the warehouse until 5:00 P.M. Maybe midnight, I thought.

Everything was running as smooth as the conditions would allow. The Nicaraguans are resourceful people and quite capable at overcoming obstacles. We were ahead of our revised schedule when the "boxed" or enclosed truck came backing in. This truck is designed to be loaded and offloaded at a dock-high facility where a forklift can drive onto the truck. How were we going to get the pallets out that the forklift couldn't reach?

A rope! Someone got the idea of tying a rope to the pallet and then to the forklift. The plan was to pull the pallet back to the rear of the truck so the forklift could reach it. Sounded good to me! The rope was attached to the forklift and the pulling began. The rope became taut and started making that sound which said, "I'm not up to this!" Everyone headed for cover. The tires on the forklift began spinning in the gravel, when all of a sudden a loud, "This-is-not-the-way-it's-supposed-to-sound" noise came from inside the truck. The rope had chewed into the wooden pallet making it a candidate for the toothpick factory. Worse yet, all the supplies on the pallet were all over the truck. The pallets were too heavy. Trying for an hour to come up with a workable plan, someone said the rope idea would work if we raised the forks higher, lifting the front of the pallet as it was being pulled. It worked!

Again, we were rolling along. It was midnight. A couple more hours and we would be finished. Then, without warning, all of the lights went out. Hey, we were in Nicaragua. You expect nothing except the unexpected. Now what were we going to do? We still have six trucks to offload. This didn't faze the Nicaraguans. They asked us to pull our cars onto the lot, face the unloading area, and turn on our headlights. By car light, the last pallets were secured in the warehouse. It was 5:00 A.M. We had been at it for nineteen hours. We thanked the drivers and workers and gave them a little money and some school supplies for their children. We were exhausted but felt a sense of accomplishment.

As the sun started to rise and the birds outside my bedroom window high in the branches of the mango trees began screaming at each other, I thanked the Lord for the day. In a span of fourteen days and nineteen hours, a warehouse was emptied and over 100,000 pounds of supplies were airlifted to an impoverished people thousands of miles away where another warehouse was filled to capacity. I thought about how when God wants something done, it gets done—but always in *His* time, not ours. We are merely threads of a great tapestry; He is the master weaver. Each thread must be woven in just the right place at just the right time. If we keep our faith, He will remain faithful. It is true. Miracles do occur at the intersection of our faith and God's faithfulness.

Four days later I arrived back in Cincinnati. My body was tired but my spirit was renewed. A few days previously I had thought the Matthew 25: Ministries dream was not shared by God. Then God led me to Captain McGregor and the issue of transportation to Nicaragua was solved. It is always in God's time. Such an important lesson, yet one so difficult to learn.

Again, that spiritual truth was so evident. When we receive a big "no," God has for us an even bigger "yes". If we get what we want, when we want it, from the people we want it from, then that's all we get. But if we keep looking, seeking, and knocking, we receive more at a better time from the people we would have never met if we got it in our time and way. Sure we are disappointed and can get discouraged, but in the end, it will be much better. Jesus said we often ask for a stone thinking it's what we need to feed our children. But Jesus said God will only give us bread. How many times have I mistaken a stone for a loaf of bread! This trip was certainly the bread. I learned so much and met some of the people who would make over thirty future airlifts possible. My next assignment was to secure another warehouse and begin filling it.

The rental market in Cincinnati was still "soft." There was another warehouse available in the same complex at a very good rate. It was double the size of our last warehouse and double the rent. I did not want to find myself in the same situation. This time I got a two year lease with an extension.

That night I told Mickey that I had just signed a two-year lease for $57,000. Our personal funds were almost depleted and contributions to Matthew 25: Ministries were just a trickle. I had committed us for almost $60,000 of money we didn't have. What's more, we had an empty warehouse and no one contributing supplies to us on a regular basis. I stood in the empty warehouse one night thinking, *How will we ever fill this place?*

Chapter Seventeen

We Can Care for a Needy World with the Things We Throw Away

I asked Tom, a man who regularly volunteered with his two sons at the warehouse, if he knew where we could find first-aid supplies. He said that he wasn't sure but he would look. Six months later he located a company and a name. He said he had been down so many blind alleys and almost gave up when someone, who knew someone, who . . . (you know how that goes) gave him a name to call. "You're never going to believe this," he said. "The company's offices are across the street from our warehouse." *Gee*, I thought, *what's God up to?* I contacted the person and we began to receive first-aid supplies from the company's distribution center in Northern Kentucky.

One morning I received a call from the company. They had several pallets of supplies for us, but they wanted them picked up that afternoon. I borrowed a pickup truck and made my way to their distribution center. Once there, I couldn't believe the volume of products they were processing on a daily basis. *Oh Lord, we certainly could use these products*, I prayed. A young man came up to me and introduced himself. He said he was sorry, but they were extremely busy and I would have to wait. I found a place out of the way to sit and brood. One forkload after another carrying pallets of supplies whizzed past me. Some products were being deposited into a good-sized holding area. I stopped one of the forklift operators and inquired about them.

"They're returns," he said.

"What are you going to do with them?" I asked.

"Well," he said, wiping the perspiration from his forehead, "after we inventory them . . . you see that trash compactor . . . in they go."

"You've got to be kidding! Except for the scuffed and torn carton the products look new," I said.

"Yeah, but it costs the company too much money to repackage them so out they go. I know it looks like a lot to you, but for a company our size, it's nothing."

I immediately located the person in charge of "returns" and asked her if I could put a forty-foot trailer at one of their dock doors 24-7. All they would have to do was run their "returns" on the trailer. We would inventory all the products. Her company would save the expense of doing the inventory and also the expense of disposing of them. They would also receive a nice tax write-off. She said she would try it for three months. We've been receiving a monthly trailerload now for eight years. God had taken me to that distribution center and, during the time I thought I was wasting, God opened my eyes to the size of the production capacity of

U.S. industry and the products which go to the landfill each day.

When I tell this story and people see the volume we receive, they always say, "Oh, how wasteful." And I always respond in two ways: First, let's say you are cooking for a group of people coming to eat at your house. You do not know how many are coming or the food they like. It turns out that a lot of people come and they love your food. Pat yourself on your back. You did a good job of estimating correctly how many people would come. Regardless, you still have leftovers. The next day you informally invite folks over for leftovers. On the third day, leftovers again. Eventually, into the trash goes some of your food!

That's corporate America. Companies are not in the business of making and selling things; they are in business to make a profit! Before they begin making and selling things, the smart companies test market their products. They try to determine in advance if people will like their products and how many people will buy them. However, they never know for certain until their products hit the marketplace. And no matter how carefully they plan, they are going to have products which don't sell or get damaged—leftovers.

Corporate America is not as successful as it is by being wasteful. Those companies which are, aren't around very long. The marketplace is too competitive. Corporate leftovers are what Matthew 25: Ministries relies on. Style changes, consumer preferences, regulations, and high standards all go into creating leftovers. The United States government has even given a handsome tax incentive for companies to give their leftovers to organizations such as Matthew 25: Ministries.

Second, we need to look at corporate leftovers in a spiritual light. The U.S. is one of the largest manufacturing and consumer nations in the world. While more manufacturing jobs are going overseas, we are still a manufacture powerhouse. Manufacturing plants and distribution centers are huge and their products number in the billions. It is true, we can help a needy world with the things we throw away! We are wasteful only if we throw things away.

God has blessed the United States in so many ways. We truly live in a land of abundance. With such blessings comes an enormous responsibility, the greater of which is to help the less fortunate of the world.

I once thought of calling Matthew 25: Ministries "Third Harvest." The first harvest of our labor is for our own, the second harvest is for the poor in America and, what is left over, the third harvest for the poor of the world. A chipped bar of soap, a worn mattress, clothing improperly labeled, shoes no longer in style, incorrectly sized surgical gloves, products with scuffed labels or torn cartons, all candidates for the landfill . . . all desperately needed in the Third World. Truly a harvest for those living in the Third World.

Chapter Eighteen

More Doors Are Opened

Over the next two years Matthew 25: Ministries would become firmly established. More people were volunteering at the warehouse and sending in financial contributions. Over a twenty-month period we accumulated enough supplies to fill and empty our warehouse twelve times. Over 2.5 million pounds of supplies were shipped to Nicaragua aboard an amazing eight C-5 cargo planes. Two of our airlifts required two C-5 cargo planes. The folks at both Kelly and Wright Patterson Air Force Bases were constantly doing their part to make all of this happen. Working with the Air Force was truly one of the unexpected pleasures for me.

Items still desperately needed were hospital furniture and equipment. These items took more time and effort than any other donations. Getting them was definitely a learning experience, one which opened the floodgates for a mountain of hospital furniture, and took me back to the hospital in which both Axel and I were patients.

It all began with a meeting with the vice president of a Cincinnati hospital. I told the vice president of the conditions in the Nicaraguan hospitals and asked him if his hospital had anything we might need. He said he would check with the appropriate personnel and get back to me. Four months later, I received a phone call from a man named Buck. He was in charge of the handling and disposal of excess hospital furniture. He said that he had some physical therapy tables if we wanted them. We agreed to meet the next day at a warehouse that the hospital was leasing. After several unsuccessful attempts, he finally managed to open a large door and in we went. When he turned on the lights my eyes became the size of dinner plates. The place was filled with beds, mattresses, exam tables, patient chairs . . . everything imaginable. Tears came to my eyes.

He took me over to the six physical therapy tables. I immediately said that we would take them. He then asked, "Well, Reverend, what else would you like?"

I replied before his words cleared his lips, "I'll take it all!"

To which he said, "If you can get it out by Friday, it's yours!"

I said what I always say when given such a challenge and ultimatum, "Sure, no problem," and then I whispered to myself, *I have no idea how I'm going to do this!*

Back at the office, I telephoned a friend who headed up the traffic department of a large corporation. He gave me the name of a person in the moving business. After pleading my case and telling him my need, he donated a driver and truck for as many days as needed to empty the warehouse. Next, I needed movers!

Since we had to remove the furniture during the work week, only a few of my volunteers could help. I had to find another source of workers. At the time, I was back at the inner-city church serving as an interim pastor. I often noticed men standing around on the street corners. Some of them I knew, most I did not. I decided that I would ask them to help. My plan was simple but somewhat risky. I simply drove my van up to the corner, rolled down my window, and told them who I was. If there were any drug dealers there, I didn't want any. I then asked them if they wanted to work for the day. I said I would give them each $35 and buy their lunch. In two stops my van was full. We emptied the warehouse by Friday. An unbelievable cache of hospital furniture and equipment filled three fifty-foot moving trucks.

Since those first truckloads of furniture, we have moved out of Cincinnati hospitals and doctors' offices over two hundred semis of furniture and equipment. When one hospital closed its doors, we were the benefactors of all the "stuff" they could not sell or use at their new location. All the furniture was crammed into one wing of the hospital. The furniture had to be taken on passenger elevators three floors below, then through two hundred yards of winding hallways to our waiting trucks. We filled three semis a day for four days. We did not have the space and time to offload them at our warehouse, so we began storing them on forty-foot trailers and parking them on the lot. One time we had over thirty semis filled with hospital furniture on our lot. When the time came to ship, we had to offload the furniture into our warehouse then load it on the oceangoing cargo containers or palletize them for their trip to the air force base. There has never been a time since those first truckloads that we have not had hospital furniture in our facility.

Hearing how Matthew 25: Ministries takes such large items which most not-for-profits cannot, we began receiving calls from other area hospitals and schools. As with everything given to us, we do not know how we are going to send the furniture or when, we just take it in faith and it always gets shipped somehow.

We have been told that Matthew 25: Ministries has completely furnished every major hospital in Nicaragua and that almost every clinic and hospital has something from some Cincinnati hospital. The school furniture has also had an impact on hundreds of schools touching the lives of thousands of children.

At the end of a long day with sore backs, bruised arms, and smashed fingers, we always say, "no more furniture." But then the phone rings and we remember the Nicaraguan hospitals and all those people with no beds, mattresses, or even as much as a chair to sit on. We say, "Sure, we can pick up the furniture first thing next week!" If we provide the labor, God will provide the way. He always has!

Chapter Nineteen

Troubled Waters

To pay the bills I went back to work with the Walnut Hills Baptist Church and also became the pastor for the newly formed church which grew out of Matthew 25: Ministries, the Church of Matthew 25. The church would have its own budget and governing body and be a completely separate entity. A portion of the Milford warehouse was sectioned off for Sunday services. Through the week the chairs would be taken down, the pulpit and piano were moved aside, and the sanctuary was converted back to a warehouse. Sometimes the conversion took place immediately after the Sunday worship service when supplies needed to be readied for an upcoming airlift. We called these days "work clothes Sunday" since the members would come to the service dressed for working in the warehouse.

Our services ended at 10:30 A.M., which gave me just enough time to drive into the city for the 11:15 A.M. services. It was a physical and emotional challenge serving two churches and heading Matthew 25: Ministries. The stress of trying to keep up with everyone and everything was also taking a toll. God had blessed me with an enormous amount of renewable energy, but cursed me with a mind which never turns off and which constantly tried to tap into that energy. Both churches were experiencing modest growth and the people seemed happy. Matthew 25: Ministries was becoming established and recognized. It just might make it past that famous three-year period when most organizations are unable to sustain the initial energy and vision and fade away. It would appear that we would not be added to the "whatever happened to what's their name?" list. Then the proverbial other shoe fell.

Of all places, I was in the dumpster smashing down boxes when a feeling of dread came over me. As surely as I am writing to you, God spoke to me with that still, small voice. This time however, it was that still, *troubling* voice. I got out of the dumpster and went into the office. Patty, my first and only part-time paid staff, asked me if I was okay. I said, "Patty, we are in for something which will test us like we've never been tested before."

We were attempting to deal with three issues which were on a collision course—and about to collide. First, the landlord came calling. We had to vacate our space in five months when the lease was up. The economy was going through a bit of an upswing and several companies were willing to pay for our space, more than we were or could. Eventually those companies did not want to wait five months, so they went looking elsewhere. At the end of our lease, we went on a month-to-month basis until we could step up and sign a longer lease for more money or another business wanted our space. Having gone through this before, I did not want to have a warehouse full of supplies and be informed that we had thirty days to vacate. This was our third warehouse. It was here, just nine months before, that we celebrated shipping our one millionth pound of supplies. It had served us well, even though we had only two docks and less than ten thousand square feet of warehouse. We were growing and we needed a large facility. It was time to go, but where?

Second, we made the decision that we would build our own facility. We had a successful financial campaign, but fell short of the money we needed to build. We had a decision to make. We could keep moving from warehouse to warehouse until we raised the needed money or build the facility ourselves. There were a few in the church who were opposed to doing this. They loudly raised questions in public which I then raised to God in private. Building our own facility was a huge risk. No one in our group had ever undertaken such a project. We had a lot of folks who possessed construction skills, but none who had ever served as a general contractor. Also, what we could afford to build on the two acres donated to us was only five thousand more square feet larger than our current warehouse. I was as frightened with the thought of doing this ourselves as opponents of the idea were angry—so much so that they left the church.

The third issue was having a paid staff. I could see that a paid staff was needed to supplement the work of the unpaid volunteers. I also knew that I could not hold down three jobs without help from someone whom I could count on to be there on a regular basis. Matthew 25: Ministries was no longer a group of people lending a hand on the weekends or in the evening. It had become a good-sized business, working with businesses Monday through Friday. I had to make a decision; hold to our initial goal of an all-unpaid volunteer organization which could only grow just so big and reach just so many people, or say people are more important than goals, and then staff to handle the growth God was giving us. My first two staff members were an administrative assistant and a forklift operator.

Our ranks were thinned; our two-acre building site was strewn with rocks of all sizes; the equipment we purchased needed tune-ups; and one piece, a complete overhaul. It rained when it wasn't supposed to and was cold when it was supposed to be warm. The city's water line was discovered where it shouldn't have been, and subcontractors' showed up for work drunk or didn't show up at all. I discovered that Mr. Murphy did not only reside in Nicaragua, but also at 1425 Loveland-Madeira Road. Each night driving home, I could hear a faint whisper, *We told you so!*

Twelve long problem-filled months later, we had an attractive, well-built facility that has served us well to this day. We built it for $400,000 lower than our lowest outside bid. I think God wanted us to build this to show others what a small, poorly financed group of people could do if they put their hand to the plow and didn't look back. Too often we have others do what we can do for ourselves. We at Matthew 25: Ministries needed to practice what we preached—self-reliance. This was what we were trying to help the poor develop. I was so proud of those who hung in there, didn't give up hope, and stuck it out to the very last brick. We finally had our own warehouse in Loveland.

During the construction period, Matthew 25: Ministries grew so rapidly that we also kept the space we leased while building the Loveland facility. Our warehouse needs required over thirty thousand square feet. We soon celebrated sending our ten millionth pound. In spite of the construction and controversy, the work of Matthew 25: Ministries was not deterred. I felt God's hand on our work more than ever. It was a difficult time, but I was constantly sustained by that little verse, "This too shall pass." It did. It always does.

Chapter Twenty

Reaching Those at Home

We were now operating out of both the Loveland facility and the space we were leasing in the old Ford plant now called the Red Bank Road Distribution Center. The place was dirty and either cold or hot (depending on the season). The building was huge, almost 600,000 square feet. In its heyday, thousands of Ford employees made transmissions there; now it housed a few small businesses but was mostly used as a storage and distribution center for numerous companies. The rent was reasonable and we could have more or less space with only a couple of weeks' notice. The one real drawback was the location of the docks. They were on the other end of the building. They were also outside, which meant we had to load and offload in the bitter cold of winter and the sweltering heat of summer. It was hard on our staff, volunteers, and on our forklifts which seemed to never stop running back and forth.

I always wanted Matthew 25: Ministries to be a place where people could be a part of a hands-on effort to help the needy. Volunteers would always be an important part of the work. I applied for and received a grant from a foundation for a volunteer coordinator, which enabled me to bring onto staff someone who would oversee the volunteer program and be in charge of processing of supplies. It was as if God was waiting for us to be ready. Soon after this person was in place, the volunteers began coming in by the carloads. Word was spreading that there was this big, wonderful place which received tons of donated goods for the poor and volunteers were desperately needed. Wearing sweaters and gloves in the winter; cooled only by fans in the summer; people came, endured the conditions, and worked only for the reward of knowing that because they came that day someone tomorrow would be helped.

This was also the time when we began receiving our first huge donation of supplies. A clothing manufacturer shipped us thirty-eight semis filled with almost 400,000 articles of new clothing, including over fifty thousand winter coats. A few months before, one of my directors, Paul Francis, brought to me his concern for American Indians. After a thorough search, we found an effective organization working with American Indians in Arizona and South Dakota. Our first shipment to them was a semiload of these new, warm winter jackets. The criticism I've received most about Matthew 25: Ministries was not doing anything for people in the U.S. I always wanted to help people everywhere, but God had called me to Nicaragua. When God called me to the U.S. and gave me the supplies, I would follow those orders as well. With this shipment of coats came the supplies, and I received new marching orders. Other than a few small charitable organizations in Cincinnati, this was the first door that opened to Matthew 25: Ministries to help the needy in the United States.

Another reason we ship overseas is because we are instructed to do so by the corporations who donate to us. These corporations do not want their products showing up at some flea market or being sold in the U.S., thus under-cutting their retail customers. Even with those winter coats, we could only ship within the U.S. if we took off the tags from every single coat—over fifty thousand of them. This was the only condition we placed on this donation and the American Indians complied.

Six months later, we received our largest one-time donation. An internationally known shoe company was closing down its Cincinnati operation and contacted us about a donation of shoes. What began as a donation of 200,000 pairs of shoes grew to almost one million pairs. They came in boxes that held a dozen to eighteen pairs of new shoes. When the trucks arrived, they were "floor loaded." This meant the boxes were not on pallets which could be offloaded with a forklift, but had to be offloaded by hand, one box at a time. Over sixty semis of shoes were offloaded, sorted according to style, palletized, and placed in inventory. All of the trucks were also "live loads," which meant that we had to unload them immediately because the truck drivers were waiting. We were offloading as many as seven trucks a day. There were so many boxes of shoes, even the additional space I had rented was not sufficient. We were forced to run them onto forty-five forty-foot storage trailers and park them on our lot. The American Indians held shoe distribution events on many of the reservations. Many of the elders, who wore only flip-flops so that their grandchildren could buy shoes, received new shoes. For many, this was their first new pair of shoes ever. I could only think of my many trips to a remote village in Nicaragua.

Of all the things I saw during my trips to Nicaragua, the one thing that stayed with me was the feet of the shoe-less. Feet which were dirty, calloused, cut and bloody from working the fields and walking those dusty roads. Each time a container filled with shoes destined for some Central American country would leave our docks, I would see in my mind a man, a child, a mother putting on perhaps their only pair of shoes, certainly the only pair of new shoes they had ever owned. I also heard Jesus say, if I may paraphrase, "When I was shoeless, you gave me a pair of shoes."

We were now a comfortable size. We were regularly sending supplies to the American Indians and soon to Appalachia. We were shipping into the war-torn Balkan countries and to over twenty different countries besides Nicaragua. We were paying our own bills, the number of volunteers was growing, and the supplies kept pouring in. Then the telephone rang. As a person of faith I can only see it as the providential hand of God; even now I get goose bumps when I think of it.

Chapter Twenty-one

The Big Storm

On the other end of the phone was a reporter who had heard about us and wanted to see if there was a story here. He visited our facilities and we talked back and forth for several days. He finally said that he got approval from his editor to do the story. When his editor read the story, he decided to run the story in the citywide section of the paper instead of just in the section for our area of the city. The article took up half a page and, for the first time, the story of Matthew 25: Ministries was told to a citywide audience. Our phones began to ring; additional people wanted to volunteer and support us financially.

A few months later I was off to Nicaragua. For many frustrating reasons, we had not been able to ship out supplies for almost a month. Our warehouse was packed. I don't like supplies to just sit in our warehouse. There are so many people who can't wait, they need help now. The focus of the trip to Nicaragua would be on the schools. We spent our

time visiting one school after another, talking with teachers
and discussing ways Matthew 25: Ministries could help. All
the time we were in Nicaragua, we kept hearing reports of a
storm in the Atlantic that was heading for the Gulf of
Mexico. The night before we were to leave, the vice president
of the country, Enrique Bolanos, invited us to dine at his
home. We had donated supplies to a Nicaraguan organization which helped children and the elderly. His wife, Lila,
and a group of her friends headed up the organization. They
wanted to thank us and discuss how we could do more
together. It was a delightful evening and we were soon back
in our hotel rooms packing to leave in the morning.

When we got to the airport, all the talk was about the
storm—now a hurricane—moving northwestward along the
Honduras border. For the first time, we flew to Nicaragua
aboard a different airline. Our normal route home was
northeast through Florida, but this time our flight was
northwest through Texas. The only plane leaving was ours.
The position of the storm gave us a few-hour window for our
departure. If we had flown the other airline we would have
been unable to leave. Climbing to ten thousand feet, the
pilot told us we could see the storm to the right side of the
plane. It was an awesome mixture of white and grey clouds
which extended in all directions as far as we could see.

Back home, we learned that the hurricane was named
Mitch and initial reports were not good. It took us at least
two days before the full impact and intensity of Hurricane
Mitch could be appreciated. It was the worst hurricane to
hit Central America in three centuries. The two countries
hardest hit were Honduras and Nicaragua. Five feet of rain
fell in forty-eight hours. Thousands were killed and

hundreds of thousands were left homeless.

For me the story which best describes the tragedy and magnitude of the storm was told to me by a friend who was working at one of the relief centers set up throughout Nicaragua. She said that each evening as new people came in, they would be encouraged to talk through the ordeals they faced.

A nine-year-old boy said that he was playing after the storm when he heard something. He went and told his parents who were shoveling mud out of their house. They told him that he was hearing the helicopters rushing relief supplies up and down the valley. They sent him back outside to play. He went out and climbed a tree. The noise he heard was the side of the Volcano Casita giving way, sending a tidal wave of mud, fifteen- to twenty-feet deep, one-half-mile wide, rushing down the valley. His entire village was covered with mud, killing every living creature. The mud toppled the tree he was in. He landed feet first and was stuck in the mud up to his waist until rescuers freed him two days later. In a matter of a few moments, his family and entire village were gone—everything killed, suffocated by a sea of mud.

I contacted the embassy in Nicaragua and my friends in the military. I now understood why we had a warehouse full of supplies. We were staging them for a hurricane before it was even a tropical depression. To my disappointment, I was told that "little" organizations like ours would not be permitted to send supplies, only the larger relief agencies. I told them that we worked in the country and already had a distribution network established. The ambassador said, "no"! I then heard that Vice President Bolanos had been appointed by the president of Nicaragua to head up the hurricane relief effort. He told me when we left his home to call him if I needed his help. He even gave me his home number, which I called. I told him that I had relief supplies available for immediate departure, but he would have to open the door for Matthew 25: Ministries, which he did. The Air Force and Department of Defense contacted me and said, "It's a go!" Within four days we had supplies to Nicaragua and to those in need!

But now our warehouse was empty, where were we going to get additional supplies? Remember the news article on Matthew 25: Ministries? The news media and people remembered it. Film crews began crawling all over our Red Bank facility. The handling and processing of supplies were definitely Kodak™ moments for television news. Corporations and the public began to send and bring in supplies. We were operating seven days a week, twelve hours a day. People just showed up saying they wanted to do something. There was this unbelievable outpouring of concern by the American people. They recognized this to be one of the greatest world tragedies of their lifetime. Six months later we had filled ten USAF cargo planes and fifty forty-foot containers. We shipped over seven hundred tons of hurricane-relief aid.

A news article, a trip to Nicaragua, a dinner with the vice president, him being appointed to head up the relief effort, first time traveling to Nicaragua on a different airline, a warehouse full of supplies . . . providence or chance?

Matthew 25: Ministries was now a household name to many of the people in the city. No longer would we be a comfortable size. We were just about ready to take another great leap of faith.

Chapter Twenty-two

Searching for a Home of Our Own

The working conditions at the old Ford plant were getting worse. One day we began smelling something in our section of the building. The heating system was emitting fumes. We were assured by management that the fumes, while they had a pungent odor, were not toxic. I was unconvinced, so I shut down our operation until the heating system was repaired.

Even more troubling to me was the stealing. Anything left on the dock or in an unsecured room was fair game. The thieves even climbed a twenty-foot wall that we installed and helped themselves to dozens of pairs of new shoes. Cameras were installed, but that did not deter the thieves. Disgusted, I put up a big sign: "You are stealing from the poor!" Their attitude or their justification for the stealing was, "They are going to give it away anyway, why not to us!" It was believed that the thieves were those who worked in the building at night. Even at minimum wage, working in such a place, they still were living like kings in America compared to the people who lived in Haiti or Nicaragua and who so desperately needed what they were stealing.

The working environment, the inability to secure our space, the arrangement of the docks, and the general "uncleanliness" of the building made it necessary for us to move. The affordable rent and the expandable space were certainly hard to leave, but I had to think of the safety and welfare of the staff and our volunteers. But where could we go? I had searched the city over before finding the Ford plant. Sharing this with one of my directors, he said that if I could make it work, we could move into an old defunct department store just down the street. He had just purchased it with a partner. It only had a few docks and we would have to make some modifications. After touring the building, I said, "We'll take it."

Later I took some of the staff down to see the new facilities. After the tour we went to our car. I said, "See that building there with all those docks? That's the building I wish we could get! It's 78,000 square feet . . . but it's too expensive for us." We drove on.

We immediately began storing hospital and school furniture at the new building. Saturday work parties were scheduled. We took up old carpeting, tore down walls, and worked on the electric. Little by little we were turning a department store into a warehouse. The biggest problem was how and where to install additional docks. I solicited the help of several architects and engineers. They told me that it could be done, but with much difficulty and at considerable cost. We were used to "difficulty," but "considerable cost," that's what I didn't like to hear.

While trying to turn this sow's ear into a silk purse, we received a call from one of our corporate donors. They had some new products they wanted to donate. Someone would have to go to their distribution center and check them out. I usually don't do this myself, but for some reason I decided to go.

I drove to a large industrial park northwest of the city, located not too far from our Circle Freeway. The area is what I call "background" scenery. You see it as you drive by, but you never really notice it until you have to go there. It took me a while, but I finally found the correct entrance. Once inside, I began asking people if they knew the whereabouts of the person I was to meet. After locating him, he took me to the shipping area. There I was shown the product in question. He excused himself after being paged and said he would be right back. Twenty minutes later, I wondered if he had forgotten about me. I began participating in one of my favorite pastimes, looking through such places hoping to spot some additional products we need.

Rounding a corner, all that I could say was, "Oh, sweet Jesus!" There before me was the biggest warehouse I had ever seen or been in. I knew from the outside that this was a big building, but the size could not be appreciated until I was inside. The building was measured in hundreds of thousands of square feet. There were pallets upon pallets stretching to the ceiling in aisles that seemed to go on forever. There were millions and millions of bars and bottles of soap. *Oh, God, how the poor need these items,* I prayed.

Overwhelmed by the enormity of the place, thinking of how desperately the poor need such supplies, I heard those same words I heard in that emergency room, *Are not my people worthy of this?* Who are God's people and what did these words mean?

To me, God was referring to people who are destitute and lack the material necessities of life: those individuals such as the Good Samaritan, the man who was robbed, beaten, and left to die on that ancient road. They too have been left hopelessly along the roadside of life. These are the people Jesus felt compassion for. They are those who have no food or water, who have no homes or clothes, those sick and in prison, people Jesus called the "least of these." Those who have the least power and control over the things needed to maintain, not a standard of living, but life itself!

Jesus was desirous of those who are destitute—those devastated by wars, natural disasters, and disease. People who in every sense of the term are truly victims. It is nothing they did or did not do. They are poor because of where they were born. They are the afflicted, people whose suffering causes our "guts" to ache and motivates us to do all we can to end or relieve their pain.

The word "poor" occurs over one hundred times in the Old and New Testaments. It almost always refers to a person destitute of material possessions, lacking the barest necessities of life. The word is also translated as weak, needy, oppressed, impoverished, and dispossessed. The poor are the special charge of God and of God's people. *The poor are not to be forgotten.* The Old Testament says, ". . . He (God) does not forget the cry of the afflicted" (Ps. 9:12). *They are to be comforted*: ". . . For the Lord has comforted his people, and he will have compassion on the afflicted." (Isa. 49:13). *He (God) deeply cares for them and seeks to help them*: "Sing to the Lord, Praise the Lord, for He has delivered the life of the needy from the hands of evil doers" (Jer. 20:13). *God seeks social justice on their behalf*: "He (God) executes justice for the fatherless and the widow and loves the sojourner, giving food and clothing" (Deut. 10:18). There is also strong warning against those who abuse the poor (Exod. 23:3; Lev. 19:15; Isa. 1:23; Ezek. 22:7; Mic. 2:2; and Mal. 3:5).

Why did God bring me here? Why those words again? First he was saying that while we in the United States have these facilities to house and distribute products which meet every conceivable physical need we have, should there not also be such places for the poor? He was also telling me that I must think bigger!

A few weeks later I was walking the perimeter of our new department store/warehouse building with an engineer. Sitting outside the warehouse next door was a man who, as it turned out, used to be the building superintendent for the department store. After the department store closed, he began working for the flooring company now occupying the warehouse I wished we had. Seeing the M25M logo on my shirt, he said, "I know your organization. You ship supplies." I nodded my head. Pointing to the department store, he asked, "You're going in there?"

"Yes," I answered with a short-lived smile on my face. He shook his head, "Those floors in there will never hold the weight of your supplies, especially your forklifts." I immediately had an engineering firm run tests to see if he was correct. He was! Now what? I'd already given notice that we were leaving from the Ford building, and I had signed a lease on the new building!

I began driving the city once again looking for another warehouse. Staying at the Ford plant was not an option. After days of searching, the realtor with me said that he had one more place to show me. We pulled into the parking lot of the department store. "Oh no," I said. "The department store . . ."

He interrupted. "No," he said, "the building next to it. The one with all the docks."

"There's a company in there now," I said.

"Yeah," he replied, "but they are moving out next month and they would like to sublease the building. They still have a year to go on their lease."

We went inside. It was huge. "What will it cost us?" I asked, not really wanting to know. When he told me, I swallowed hard. It would be six times what we were currently paying. I remembered that other huge warehouse and the words, *"Are not my people worthy of this?"* I said, "I'll take it!"

We moved in and stayed for a year. We tried to continue to lease or even buy the building, but the price was unrealistic, so once again I went looking for a warehouse. The next warehouse would be the eighth in ten years! We had become the eight-hundred-pound gorilla. Moving was a behemoth undertaking. Before this move we shipped out forty containers in six weeks and still needed twenty-seven semis to move the supplies from the Red Bank warehouse to our new Highland Avenue warehouse.

We were in our new warehouse only six months when we passed another milestone. We shipped our twenty millionth pound of supplies in 1,250 forty-foot ocean-going containers. Forty-five thousand pallets of supplies were shipped, impacting the lives of millions of people in over thirty countries and a growing number of places in the U.S. It had taken us four years to reach one million; another four years to reach ten million; and now just two more years to reach twenty million pounds. We had a wonderful celebration.

Our twenty-four-foot truck is picking up supplies daily in a one-hundred-mile radius of Cincinnati. Corporations are now donating to us over five million pounds of supplies a year. We converted the Loveland operation into a manufacturing center where we are producing four to five thousand notebooks a day for poor children and, in the process, giving jobs to people who are trying to better their lives. The staff is growing and volunteers are increasing. We are booking volunteer groups three to four weeks ahead. Each day is a new discovery, challenge, and blessing. Every bill is paid on time—close, but never late. Facing another lease issue and the possibility of another move, my prayers are still for a home of our own. One that is large enough to reach even more of the poor in the world and the United States, and paid for so that our quarter of a million dollars yearly rent payment can go to sending more supplies helping more people. A place I could stand in and say, *Yes, Lord, your people are worthy of this and here it is!*

Chapter Twenty-three

The Jefferson Award

I was contacted in the Spring of 2003 by the newspaper and informed that I was a finalist for the Jefferson Award for Public Service. The winner would be announced at a downtown luncheon the following week. *What's the Jefferson Award?* I wondered.

The Jefferson Award was founded in 1972 by Sam Beard, Jacqueline Kennedy Onassis, and a U.S. senator from Ohio, Robert Taft. Together they began the American Institute for Public Service, which is a bipartisan national organization whose purpose is to recognize people throughout the United States for their public service. Each year over ninety people are selected by local committees to receive the Jefferson Award medallion. The recipients are invited to go to Washington, D.C., for the national ceremonies.

Mickey and I attended the luncheon and had the honor and privilege of sitting with the other finalists. They were wonderful people engaged in many worthy causes. While each of them were introduced, I tried to guess which one of them was going to receive the award. There was one person I thought was definitely going to win. When the envelope was opened and out popped my name, I was speechless. The next thing I remembered was that I was at the podium with the beautiful Jefferson Award medallion in my hands. They told me that my acceptance remarks were memorable; maybe so, but I don't remember them. It was all just a blur. The next day a wonderful article about the award and Matthew 25: Ministries appeared in the newspaper.

The next week we received a packet of information about the Jefferson Award and an invitation to attend the National Ceremonies. A few weeks later, a film crew came to Cincinnati and spent an entire day interviewing and taking videos of everyone connected with Matthew 25: Ministries. They said that they were traveling the country visiting a number of recipients. All the time I was in front of the camera, not one of my favorite places, I kept reminding myself that this national exposure would be good for Matthew 25: Ministries and, bottom line, it will help the poor! They left and I didn't think anything more about their visit.

The event in Washington was impressive. The accommodations were great, the food excellent, every conceivable detail was covered. What we enjoyed the most was meeting and getting to know the other recipients. We felt like we were a part of a wonderful club whose only membership requirement was helping others.

After the four national award recipients were announced, two of the most well known being Anne Douglas and

Condoleezza Rice, Corbin Bernsen said that now they were going to announce the Jacqueline Kennedy Onassis Award recipients. I looked over at Mickey. "What is this award?" A portion in the literature I had failed to read was that the Jefferson Award selection committee would choose from all the Jefferson Award recipients five Jacqueline Kennedy Onassis recipients. The winners were to be announced at the gala.

The lights went down and we were asked to give our attention to the two large screens. As each recipient was announced, a video of their work was shown on these big (getting bigger) screens. The way the videos were put together, and especially the way in which the people were interviewed, all looked familiar. I was becoming suspicious. Then I heard my name announced and there on those screens were the words Matthew 25: Ministries followed by a video of the people and facilities back in Cincinnati.

My good friends, Shannon and Dick, who nominated me for the award came to Washington to see me receive it. They kept it all a big secret. Dick was sitting next to me at the table. When the video ended, he turned, grinning from ear to ear, and gave me a big hug. Called to the microphone again, I don't remember what I said, but Mickey said it was well received.

The closing ceremony would be held next morning in the Kennedy Center. The four National Jefferson Award recipients and the five National Jacqueline Kennedy Onassis Award recipients would officially receive their medallions. We were all kept in a back room at the Kennedy Center until we were to go on stage. The Douglases were there. While most told Kirk Douglas how

much they enjoyed him as Spartacus, I told him my
favorite character as a boy was when he played Ulysses. He
gave me a nod and a thumbs up. When we walked onto
the stage the people stood up and applauded. After what
seemed like an eternity, my name was called. Walking to
the microphone I kept repeating, *Aim for the Heart!*

I didn't sleep much the night before. I kept thinking
about what I would say. I also was struggling with what was
appropriate for me to say regarding my faith in God and
love for Jesus who, after all, gave to me the vision, direction, and the very words of Matthew 25: Ministries. It was
for Him that I began Matthew 25: Ministries. He was my
inspiration and the One who strengthened me with His
presence and led me with the visions. Faith has become
almost a four letter word in the U.S. You can run a secular
humanitarian organization and nothing is said about
motive, but if you are a faith-based organization, you are
looked at with a great deal of suspicion. I have never used
one bar of soap, roll of bandages, or a hospital bed to pros-
elytize anyone to my belief. I was, however, never hesitant
to tell people that Jesus was the reason for Matthew 25:
Ministries. I also knew that there would be people of all
faiths in attendance and some perhaps with no faith at all.
I wanted in the prayers I gave at both dinners and now in
my acceptance speech to include everyone, but at the same
time reflect my faith. Bottom line. Should I mention Jesus
and say the words of Matthew 25:34–40?

Early that morning I took a walk seeking direction
from God. My remarks would not be written down but
well thought out. I wanted to leave room for the spirit of
God to move through my words. Maybe all of this was for

that one person sitting in the audience who could help us in our work. I turned the corner and there was this large stone building. Men were working on its roof. I stopped to watch them work. When one of the men moved, I saw chiseled in the stone the word "Church." *Oh*, I thought, *it's a church building*. The man moved again, and the name of the church was revealed—St. Matthews Church. I knew then what I was going to say.

Standing before the audience I said, "Some called him Rabbi, others Teacher, some, Lord. His name was Jesus. One day he said to twelve bewildered disciples, 'Then the King will say to those on his right, "Come, you who are blessed by my Father; take your inheritance, the kingdom prepared for you since the creation of the world. For I was hungry and you gave me something to eat, I was thirsty and you gave me something to drink, I was a stranger and you invited me in, I needed clothes and you clothed me, I was sick and you looked after me, I was in prison and you came to visit me.

"'Then the righteous will answer him, "Lord, when did we see you hungry and feed you, or thirsty and give you something to drink? When did we see you a stranger and invite you in, or needing clothes and clothe you? When did we see you sick or in prison and go to visit you?

"'The King will reply, "I tell you the truth, whatever you did for one of the least of these brothers of mine, you did for me,"' Matthew 25:34–40."

I quickly summarized what Matthew 25: Ministries does, its beginning, its growth, and the number of people helped each year. All the time telling myself, *Aim for the heart*. I closed by saying, "All of that is just numbers!"

At that moment I knew I was going to tell a story, but I didn't know which one; I left that up to God. Traveling faster than my beating heart, God took me back to one of my first visits to Nicaragua. I remembered the little baby boy who was so severely burned. Holding back the tears, I said: "When I raised my camera to take his picture, all I could see were his sad eyes looking up at me. Children should not have sad eyes. They should have happy eyes. Far too many children have seen and witnessed too many things not even grown-ups should see and witness. Too many children in this world have terrible things happen to them. Too many children have sad eyes.

"Each time I go back to Nicaragua I search the crowds for that little boy, now hopefully a young man. I am afraid I will never see those eyes again, at least not in this life. They never had the opportunity to become happy eyes. But I see him in those same sad eyes of too many children. As long as God gives me strength I will do all I can to change sad little eyes into happy little eyes."